101

"Little Things" That Can Make a BIG Difference

Developing a Consistently Successful Football Program

Lew Johnston

ISBN: 978-1-60679-073-1
Library of Congress Control Number: 2009936261
Cover design: Studio J Art & Design
Book layout: Studio J Art & Design
Front cover photo: John H. Sheally II/The Virginian-Pilot

Coaches Choice
P.O. Box 1828
Monterey, CA 93942
www.coacheschoice.com

Dedication

To my wife Nancy and our children, Bryan and Mandy, who have always been my biggest fans. And to the Glory of God.

Contents

Acknowledgments

This project could never have been completed without the support and encouragement of my wonderful wife. Thank you Nancy for proof-reading this manuscript and for your encouragement throughout the process.

Though my Mom and Dad have been gone a long time, I still appreciate the love and support they gave me while I was growing up. They instilled the work ethic and the passion in my soul that motivated me to succeed—they were the best parents ever.

To my high school coaches, Jimmy Calhoun, Harry Blevins, and, in particular, my head coach, Billy O'Brien. I send a special note of thanks to Coach O'Brien—you took an immature, young boy and helped make me a self-confident young man. You showed me what a real winner is.

I want to acknowledge Art Brandriff, my principal for all those years at Western Branch High School. He took a chance and hired me and then stood by me through those tough first five seasons. I appreciate all of your support.

Thanks to all those coaches over the years who answered my endless questions and provided ideas that helped make us so successful for so long at Western Branch. I need to extend a special note of thanks to my former "right-hand man," Brian Burke. You were the best assistant coach any head coach could ask for. I want to express my thanks to Sam Warren for bringing that "fire" that we were lacking in our program until you arrived. Though you were on our staff for only a short stint, you have continued to impact my life over the years.

I send a big "praise God" to all of the men who served as our unofficial "Team Chaplains" over the years: Rick Lawrenson, Jim Wall, Michael Strickland, Keith Lowry, Jason Williams, Melvin Marriner, and Paul Richard. Thank you for being there for the players and for me.

To all those players whom I coached for 34 years—you made it all worthwhile. All the hours spent together in the weight room, on the practice field, and on the sideline were the best times of my professional life. It was great being a Bruin.

Finally, I want to thank God for giving me the opportunity to work with and minister to so many people during my 22 years as head football coach at Western Branch High School. "God is good…all the time!"

Foreword

I first met Lew Johnston about 15 years ago when I started recruiting at Western Branch High School. What started out as a business relationship forged itself into a friendship based on mutual respect and trust. Lew has always gone the extra mile for his program, school, players, family, and faith. He has consistently sought out information and new ideas to improve all facets of his program, in the hopes of helping young men reach their potential. Over the years, Lew and I have spent countless hours on the phone and in person bouncing ideas off of each other. I am pretty sure that our wives did not share in our zeal to "save" the game.

In *101 Little Things That Can Make a BIG Difference*, Lew Johnston has presented a blueprint for success for coaches of all ages and experience levels. He has managed to use his experience as a highly successful high school coach and teacher to document and present the daily, weekly, and yearly musts that any coach would value as a reference and resource. Coupled with his organizational skills and keen attention to details, he has been able to offer a plan from A to Z for all those who aspire to be a part of the coaching profession. This book is a detailed endeavor that identifies and illustrates all the "little things" that allow the "big things" to occur. From bettering yourself, your staff, your program, and your players, this book affords all of us the opportunity to have success and to maintain that success both on and off the field.

Lew and I once talked at length about a disagreement we were having in regard to the recruiting process. We finally realized that in order for our friendship to continue to grow, we were going to have to "agree to disagree" and let it go. One element that leaves no room for disagreement is that this book captures and outlines all the components necessary for professional growth and success.

What a great legacy Coach "J" has left in terms of being a coach, a mentor, and as a friend to so many. What a great opportunity he has given to all of us to pursue our dreams and aspirations to the fullest.

Thanks my good friend,
Bryan Stinespring, Offensive Coordinator
Virginia Tech

Introduction

There were so many things that I learned over the 22 years of my head coaching tenure that proved to be invaluable in our success that to enumerate on all of them would take way too long. While "X's and O's" and the level of talent are essential to any football program's success, I have come to realize that it was the *little things* that I emphasized, which made a BIG difference.

One of the two major foundation blocks in building a successful high school football program is establishing your own coaching philosophy—how you will conduct your program and present yourself to your players, your coaches, the players' parents, and the general public. For example, my philosophy is one of "tough love." I wanted my players to know that I cared about them, not only as football players but also as young adults. But, I also wanted them to know that I had high expectations for them and would exhort, correct, and teach them to achieve their highest level of success on and off the field. In essence, I wanted to motivate out of love, not fear. When players know that you want to help them succeed, they will rally around you and your program. To build support and belief in your program, you have to show people that you will cooperate, challenge, and care for them.

The other foundation block of any successful program is *organization*. I have a slogan that exemplifies what I tried to institute throughout my 22 years at the helm. I call it "The 5 P's of Success:"

Proper Preparation Prevents Poor Performance

I totally disagree with the old saying that "practice makes perfect." The only type of practice that produces anything close to perfection is *perfect* practice. Too many people tend to equate activity with achievement. You can work at something for hours and days at a time but accomplish little in the end. Why? Because you have not been practicing the correct techniques. Good coaches of successful programs *know* their subject and teach it in such a way that their players are prepared to execute those techniques on game night to the best of their ability. Knowing those techniques and motivating your players to consistently utilize them beyond their normal ability range is the mark of a great coach.

Attention to detail is another important concept to stress to your players and staff. I wanted our players to develop the attitude of "been there...done that," which means that your players have been prepared to deal with any situation that may arise during a game. As a coach, you have anticipated those plays that can turn a game around (i.e., knowing when a kick can be returned and when it can only be downed) in your favor. One of the highest compliments our team received from an opposing coach was when he said, "If you make a mistake against Lew's team, they are going to take advantage of it." Those are the foundation blocks—the bedrock, in my mind, of building a successful program.

The previously mentioned coaching philosophy that we lived by was based on three cornerstones: Unity, pride, and total effort. We worked relentlessly to develop these three traits in all of our players. Our success as a team was predicated on the level of unity we achieved as a team; how much pride our players exhibited in the success we obtained (like the craftsman who makes a beautiful piece of furniture); and the knowledge that we had to exhibit a *total* effort every day if we were going to be a championship football team.

I also believed in what I heard a coach once call the "double victory." We wanted our players to be successful on *and* off the field. We had expectations for their conduct in school and around our community. My focus was just as much on helping our players develop a sense of maturity and respect for others as it was on tackling a ballcarrier to the ground. I would not have been satisfied with just a championship football team if we were not also recognized in our community as being a group of good citizens, which is a responsibility that every high school coach should take very seriously.

Thus, it becomes the *little things* that go into constructing the framework of this "house." Winning programs train their players to do the things that make the difference between a functional home and a mansion. In this book, I will provide a short explanation of each of the *little things* that we incorporated into our program. This list is presented in sections that cover the entire year. Each *little thing* is significant in building a program that wins on a consistent basis over a long period of time.

As I gained knowledge of these *little things* and incorporated them into our program, our record improved significantly. From the sixth year of my head coaching tenure in 1991 until I retired after the 2006 season, we had one season at five and five. For the other 15 seasons, we were undefeated (10-0) three times; nine and one four times, and eight and two six times. We were fortunate enough to win five district championships and one regional championship during that period. We made it to the state semi's one year, losing in double overtime. At one point, from the 2001 season until the 2004 season, we won 32 straight regular-season contests. We were very successful over a long period of time because we implemented these *Little Things That Can Make a BIG Difference* and kept emphasizing these things year after year. We were not blessed with an abundance of talent but we developed our players by utilizing these *little things* to the point that we believed in ourselves, our coaches, and each other.

1

Staff Organization

Finding quality assistant coaches seems to be more and more of a problem every year. Many assistant coaches do not teach at the school. Instead, head coaches are talking to coaches in the community leagues and other areas to be able to hire quality people who know football and care about kids. If you can recruit quality volunteer coaches from the community and work out a means of dividing the pay supplement that the school system offers football coaches, you can hire good people and at least offer those individuals a partial supplement. If you are considering bringing in an unpaid volunteer coach with only rec-league-level experience, be sure to have an in-depth interview to find out his knowledge of the game and his coaching philosophy and attitude toward children/teens. Putting together a first-rate staff is critical to a team's success, but developing that staff once it is solidified produces the biggest rewards. A head coach has to win the respect of his assistant coaches as well as his players. The best way to achieve this respect is to be organized and knowledgeable of all aspects of the program.

#1: Staff Duties

It is critical that staff members have a clear understanding of what their on-field and off-field duties are. They need to learn of their responsibilities early in the summer. Once responsibilities are laid out, a coach has no excuse for not getting his jobs done. Having these responsibilities written down holds each coach accountable to the head coach and the rest of the team. Living in such a media-driven society, where everyone is vying for recognition, giving each coach a "title" will motivate him to work harder for the team, especially if he is not being paid for his time. Figure 1-1 provides a sample list of coaching staff title assignments.

Staff Assignments

Lew Johnston
• head coach
• offensive coordinator

Mike Santomauro
• assistant head coach
• defensive ends
• offensive tight ends
• video coordinator

Eric Santomauro
• defensive coordinator
• kickoff team coordinator
• defensive tackles
• offensive line (assist MacVey)

Charles Thomas
• scout-team coordinator
• punt team coordinator
• split ends
• safeties

Keith Burnell
• kickoff return-team coordinator
• corners
• running backs

Ian MacVey
• PAT/FG team coordinator
• offensive line

Terry Walker
• punt block team coordinator
• outside linebackers
• fullbacks

Figure 1-1. Sample coaching staff title assignments

#2: On-the-Field Responsibilities

How you delegate responsibilities depends on how many staff members you have and the experience or knowledge level of those coaches. Also take into consideration whether a particular coach is being paid or is volunteering his time. Being paid generally puts a little more pressure on a coach to perform his duties and be accountable.

The knowledge level of assistant coaches is something that the head coach is responsible for. It is important to assign a coach to a position that he is comfortable with and has knowledge of. A head coach should never take a defensive back and make him the offensive line coach. It is important that every assistant coach knows that he will be allowed to coach his position. As head coach, you need to impress upon each of your assistants that the success on game night of those players that he personally instructs in practice rests in his hands. He must have them ready.

Another area of concern is who to assign as freshman and/or JV coach. Some coaches believe that you should take one of your best coaches and make him the head coach for the junior varsity or freshman team. A better solution is to take a young coach with a lot of energy who gets along with people and *train* him to be the head JV coach (refer to #4: Coaching the Coaches). This method will allow you to use your best coaches on the varsity team.

#3: Off-the-Field Responsibilities

It is important to assign off-the-field tasks to assistant coaches. The tendency for too many head coaches is to micromanage every aspect of the program. You have highly competent coaches who can perform a number of functions, but often the head coach doesn't call upon them to help out. Think of the nights of staying back and cleaning up the locker room and locking up everything by yourself and grumbling that nobody was around to help you finish up. All you need to do is ask for help.

At the pre-season staff meetings, present a list of off-field (as well as on-field) duties to the coaches. For the most part, everyone will accept his responsibilities graciously. You may have to follow up at times throughout the season and remind a coach that a particular duty is his responsibility; but for the most part, it relieves a lot of stress for the head coach.

Make one assistant coach responsible for locker room clean-up. That coach then designates player groups (by position) to take turns cleaning up. If the locker room doesn't pass inspection, then the coach and the designated group have to stay after practice the following night for some extra conditioning drills as a reminder to do their job correctly.

Assign another coach to assist in the equipment room. If a player needs a new chin strap, that coach has to go unlock the equipment room and get him one. For items, such as mouthpieces, that tend to get lost or damaged, the coach should charge players a fee (e.g., one dollar) to get a new one. That money can then go into a fund to help pay for player recognition awards, such as weight room plaques.

Another assistant coach should be assigned to golf-cart duty. He is in charge of getting the cart out each day, driving it to the practice field (after the managers load it up), and then returning it to the garage every night after practice. This assistant coach should also learn how to plug in the charger so it doesn't run out of battery power somewhere between the locker room and the practice field.

Look around and list all the things you need done each day to keep your program running smoothly. Assign these tasks to your assistant coaches to help relieve you to spend more time coaching football. Figure 1-2 provides a sample list of off-the-field duties and responsibilities.

Off-the-Field Duties and Responsibilities

- Waiting for parents to pick up all players before coach(s) depart
- Equipment room: organization of equipment room; handing out equipment to players in August; inventory of equipment after season
- Washing of practice and game uniforms
- Locker room: clean-up; locker and lock distribution
- Storage room: blocking dummies and other practice gear
- Weight room
- Video/computer coordination
- Carwash fundraiser coordinator
- Practice field maintenance/painting
- Grades and academic eligibility

Figure 1-2. Sample list of off-the-field duties and responsibilities

#4: Coaching the Coaches

It is the responsibility of the head coach to be sure that every assistant not only understands his coaching duties but that he can perform them in a fashion that will lead to success on the field. This duty requires the head coach to "coach the coaches." Coaching the coaches requires time spent in the off-season reviewing your offense, defense, and kicking game and going over the assistant coach's position requirements with him. Particularly for a new assistant coach, the head coach must be sure that the new coach is up to speed in all aspects of the program. Giving the new assistant written quizzes is very effective, and putting him in a classroom situation where he is responsible for answering questions about the material covered over the previous few days by the head coach is highly motivating. The grade that the assistant earns is an indicator of how interested he is in becoming a knowledgeable staff member. This coaching requires extra work on the head coach's part during the off-season, but it is a critical factor in the success that will be experienced in the fall. Figure 1-3 provides a sample coach's quiz.

Wing-T Quiz #4 (Center and Guards—80 Series)

- Who is the primary ballcarrier in the 80 series? _____
- What is the "complementary" play in the 80 series for our buck sweep (21/29)? _____
- 82/88 is run down only to which side (tight end or split end)? _____
- 83/87 is primarily run to which side? _____
- Why do we add the word "down" when we call 82 or 88 in the huddle? _____
- What is the playside guard's rule on 82/88 down? _____ - _____
- What is your backside guard's rule on 82/88 down? _____
- Although the rule is the *same* for the playside guard and tackle on 82/88 keep pass, the blocking technique changes for the pulling guard. Explain what the change is and why the change in technique has to be made. _____
- The "calls" for 83/87 have become easier to remember than their rule by our playside guard and tackle. Explain what each of the calls is and why does the guard make it.

  ✓ Call: _____ when?

  _____

  ✓ Call: _____ when?

  _____

- Which lineman makes the call on 83/87? _____
- Which lineman makes the call on 32/38? _____
- The play is fly 487 keep pass and the call at the line is "jumbo" by the guard. What technique will your 7 tackle use to block the defensive end? _____
  What will the guard do? _____
- When we want to use one of our 50-series patterns in our keep passes (hawk 482 keep pass "tar heel"), what changes in the pass-blocking scheme for our linemen? _____
- Simplicity = _____
- We call roll-to fly 489 down sweep. Explain how just hearing the "suffixes" ("down" and "sweep") called in the huddle will tell our linemen what to do on this play.

  _____

- We call Hawk 482 down (quarterback) sweep. Explain as in the previous question.

  _____

- What does your playside guard think when he hears "down"? _____
- What do your guards think when they hear "trap"? _____
- What is your center's rule on 82/88 down and 83/87? _____
- Why is "gap" almost always the first rule for any playside lineman who is not pulling?

  _____

- When your tackle down blocks inside, where does he want his butt to face? And what does he have to move to accomplish this position? _____
- One of our key coaching points is "stay on your blocks!" What does the lineman have to keep moving to accomplish this? _____

Figure 1-3. Sample coach's quiz

#5: Pre-Season Staff Meetings

Some head coaches choose to take the staff away for the weekend prior to practice starting. They can play some golf, cook out, or just hang out, in addition to preparing for the season. The staff is together and a lot can be accomplished. If going on a retreat is not feasible, however, then stay home and conduct your meetings on three consecutive nights (for two hours each night) the week before practice starts. Close the weight room and give the players a chance to get away for a week while the coaches meet to get the last details nailed down before practice starts.

During the pre-season staff meetings, each coach should get up in front of the staff and present the drills he will use in his individual practice period (refer to Figure 1-4 for a sample position coach drill sheet). (Each coach should present his drills to the head coach in private before this staff meeting to be sure that he is properly prepared.) The rest of the staff act as the "players" that he walks through the drills, and after the presentation, they should critique and give feedback to the presenter. It is up to each coach to take these suggestions and have his drills ready for the first practice.

Player policies and season goals should be reviewed. Discuss coaches' policies as to conduct and expectations (refer to Figure 1-5 for a sample of coaching staff policies and guidelines). A copy of the first week's practice schedule should also be presented to each coach at the last meeting of the pre-season week. It should be a working copy stating exactly what you want to accomplish each day of that first week of practice. Have a daily installation list for each coach and an outline of what the pre-season practice and meeting schedule will look like. Again, "proper preparation" means keeping coaches and players informed. All questions should be answered and all details should be covered before leaving the meeting on the last night because the staff will not see each other again until an hour before the first practice the following Monday.

Position Coach Drill Sheet—Offense

Name _____

Position _____

General Fundamentals Drills per Your Position

Fundamental to be taught: _____

Description of drill: _____

_____

_____

Fundamental to be taught: _____

Description of drill: _____

_____

_____

Fundamental to be taught: _____

Description of drill:_____

_____

_____

Wing-T-Specific Drills per Your Position

Wing-T skill to be taught: _____

Description of drill:_____

_____

_____

Wing-T skill to be taught: _____

Description of drill:_____

_____

_____

Wing-T skill to be taught: _____

Description of drill:_____

_____

_____

Figure 1-4. Sample position coach drill sheet

Football Coaching Staff Policies and Guidelines

The following information is designed to help each of us understand our responsibilities as coaches; to promote team/staff unity; and to maintain order. As football coaches, high expectations are set for our success on the field and our conduct off the field. Every coach must abide by the following policies. Just as we expect certain behaviors from our players, we must demand the same high level of integrity and discipline from our coaches.

- *Be honest.* Nothing breaks down trust quicker than finding out that someone has lied or misled you. Our communication must be respectful of each other at all times—even when we don't agree. If you have a concern about something, you have a responsibility to bring it to my attention. Talking behind someone's back is unacceptable.
- *Be on time.* Punctuality is a sign of discipline and respect for others. We expect the players to be on time, and we must do the same. In fact, we should be early. Coaches should be at the stadium before the players start arriving for practice or games. Staff meetings will begin on time and end on time. We need everyone there so we can work together.
- *Leaving.* Please check in with me before you leave every day. There may be something that I need to cover with you before you head out. Let me know ahead of time if you have to leave early. On game nights, we will have a brief staff meeting after the players have left. Then, all coaches will need to pitch in and help clean up before anyone is excused to leave the locker room.
- *No profanity.* Refraining from profanity is a sign of discipline—plus, I find it offensive. We are role models for the players and it does not set a good example if they hear us using street language like they do in so much of society. Be careful during games—especially if you are in the press box. Fans are sitting just below and can hear most everything you say.
- *Sportsmanship.* It is critical that we show respect to opposing coaches, players, and officials. Our players are taking their cues on how to act based on the way they see us interact with others. I *never* want our players and/or coaches to give people a reason to criticize our behavior.
  - ✓ As head coach, it is my firm belief that we are not here to belittle opponents by "running up the score" on them. I will consult you as to who you think should get to play; but I will be the *final authority* on when we start sending substitutes into the game, who plays, and what position they go in to play. There are times when statistical ratings simply have to be given up for the sake of the players. If they are attending practice every day and participating, they deserve the chance to get on the field during a blow-out. Think about how you would feel if it was your son who never got to play.
  - ✓ *Note*: If a fight breaks out during the game, NO coaches are to go on the field! Our job is to keep our players on the sideline.
- *Sideline conduct.* No one will speak to the officials except the head coach. We cannot afford to get a 15-yard penalty because you commented about an official. We also cannot afford to get a reputation of bad-mouthing officials. We've gotten our share of breaks because the officials who work our games consider our coaches and players to be people who conduct themselves properly during a game. Only three coaches are allowed in the box at any time during the game. With so many coaches on the sideline, it is going to be important that you exhibit self-control and stay behind the line if that is where you are assigned.
- *Alcohol, drugs, and tobacco products.* I cannot dictate to you what you do on your own time but we must, again, set a good example when we are representing the school. Be careful of what you say (or don't say) when talking to the players about the use of these substances. We must abstain from drinking or smoking around the players and discourage them from doing the same. Obviously, the use of *illegal* substances is totally unacceptable!

Figure 1-5. Sample football coaching staff policies and guidelines

- *Coach/parent relationship.* Our relationship with our players' parents is an important part of maintaining our family atmosphere. Obviously, we can't please all of the parents, because not everyone on the team can start or be the star. We can, however, show respect for the parents' feelings. I would also appreciate it if you, as an assistant coach, would be something of a buffer for me in dealing with parents who approach you with a concern or complaint.
- *Closed practices.* Our practice field is our classroom. We will conduct ourselves as professionals at all times. Please dress appropriately for practice and conduct your sessions with enthusiasm and intelligence. Come to practice properly prepared to instruct. Your ability to be an effective time manager will be critical to your teaching success. There will always be a general-practice schedule. But I will give you the autonomy (and responsibility) to be prepared to teach your position's players the skills and drills that you feel are necessary to keep us at the championship level. Parents, friends, and such are not allowed at our practices, thus we can conduct them as a classroom session. Learn to "coach on the run." When we are in a team period, we won't always be able to stop and hold everyone up while one player is corrected. Be active and involved—especially when we are doing a team period. The team period is *not* the time to take a break.
- *Injuries.* Treatment of injuries is not our responsibility as coaches. That is what our medical staff is trained to do. Do *not* belittle a player if he is injured and is held out of practice—be an encourager. I'm not saying that we "baby" the injured player, but we need to understand that injuries are part of the game. Embarrassing him to get him back on the field does not help anyone. Help the player to know that we miss him and need him back as soon as the trainer releases him.
- *Player/coach relationship.* We have a responsibility to our players and their parents to teach our players the game of football as well as the game of life. There are so few strong, positive role models in society today. Your players look up to you, whether you realize it or not. I would not have hired you if I didn't think that you were in the game for the kids. We need to treat them with respect, while at the same time, handing out *tough love* when necessary. Correct mistakes, but try to be as positive and encouraging as you can. Solidly-built relationships are based on mutual respect and admiration. We want our kids to *want* to come out for football because they want to play for us.
- *Staff loyalty.* Although the other points in this list are all important, this one is pretty much the *foundation* of any successful organization. Without a sense of allegiance and devotion to our program, we are doomed to failure. As your head coach, I have to know that I can count on each of you to protect my back—as well as me, yours. As members of this staff, each of us must know that we can depend on one another. There must be an unwavering, firm commitment to remain true to our program's philosophy. I need to know that I can count on you to stand together with me when the times get tough. If someone criticizes a coach, a player, or our program in general, it is your responsibility to *speak up* in our defense. (Silence is often assumed to be *agreement* with the person who criticized.) We must be confident that each of us will pull his share of the load and that we can count on you to rise up when your best is needed.

Lew Johnston
Head Football Coach

Figure 1-5. Sample football coaching staff policies and guidelines (cont.)

#6: Pre-Season Coaches' Get-Together

It is important that you create opportunities to build staff unity. Staff unity is just as important as team unity. As the head coach, you can build unity and develop loyalty from your staff by going out of your way to show your appreciation for the hard work and time they devote to your program. This activity should be conducted regardless of your win-loss record. Letting people know you recognize their contributions is critical to keeping the staff happy and cooperative. Some examples of enjoyable occasions that promote team unity include taking the staff out to lunch the day of your last pre-season scrimmage or inviting the coaches and their wives over to your house for a cookout. Make a public "thank you" to the staff and tell them how excited you are to be going into a new season with each of them.

#7: Post-Season Get-Together and Gift

At the end of a long season, it is appropriate for the head coach to again bring the staff together for a show of appreciation for their hard work and dedication throughout the season. Taking the staff out to dinner at a local restaurant is always a favorite. At that time, you can reflect on the season, laugh about the good times, and commiserate about the bad. You should also present each staff member with a small gift. The *Successories*® catalog (www.successories.com) has inexpensive, motivational gifts to present to a staff. Let your people know that they are appreciated. Formal evaluations should be done at a later date. This get-together is just a time to say "thank you!"

#8: Staff Communication

As the head coach, it is paramount that you let your staff members know that you are available to talk. You must be prepared for a lot of moaning and groaning because most people typically want to find all the things that are wrong and sit around and complain. You must learn that you cannot allow your coaches to focus on the negatives. Be open to complaints but tell them that if they bring a problem, you want a solution brought with it.

Let your staff know that you will be open to their suggestions, but that you will not necessarily agree to implement them. One caution for any head coach is to *not* get caught up trying to find that "perfect play" that you think will win a championship for you. One play is just not that significant, and if in an attempt to find the perfect play or to keep your staff happy, you install all the new plays they come up with each week, you will have so much offense that you won't be able to be proficient in anything. Thus, the whole program suffers. Be open and *involve* your assistant coaches in daily decisions so that they will continue to offer suggestions and make good recommendations. You must, however, let them know that not everything they bring to you will be implemented.

You should know that you can expect your assistants to talk about you behind your back—it's just the nature of the beast. We live in a judgmental society. As the head coach, you have to let the criticism and second-guessing roll off your back. Have a plan and work your plan. Talk to your coaches and listen to them. Keep the lines of communication open. Figure 1-6 provides a sample post-season program evaluation.

Post-Season Program Evaluation

Coaches:

I would appreciate your input on the following questionnaire. Please respond honestly and use as much depth as you need to explain your thinking. Remember, if you have a constructive criticism, please give me a suggestion as to how we can improve. I will probably like to talk with you in person about your comments on a future date.

Please return this questionnaire to me by [date]. Thanks for your help.

–Lew

What are three strengths of our program (i.e., what do we do well)?

-
-
-

What are three things that we do *not* do well? What do we need to improve upon?

-
-
-

Take the three things that you feel we need to improve upon and give me a recommendation for each one on *how* we can make it better.

-
-
-

Figure 1-6. Sample post-season program evaluation

#9: Helping Assistant Coaches Achieve Their Career Goals

One of the roles that a head coach must accept is that of vocational advisor for your assistant coaches. Most every assistant aspires to be a head coach and run his own program one day. Even for those individuals who don't want to be a head coach, it is important to sit down with each assistant and explore his goals in coaching. A strong head coach is going to help his assistants move up the ladder in the coaching profession. To hold a coach back for selfish reasons can create a problem, which can come back to haunt you later in your own career.

Call in each assistant coach during the off-season. At this meeting, you can include an evaluation of the job he did for you during the past season. One of the main topics of conversation should be to ask him: "Where do you see yourself five years from now?" This question will provide a lot of latitude to discuss his future. You can also share your vision for him. Talk about what it's going to take for him to arrive at that place and set some goals. The most important thing is to let him know that you will do anything you can to help him achieve his goals.

Off-Season Activities

To be a successful high school football coach and to develop a winning program, it is necessary to work nearly year-round. Once you have enjoyed your year-end team banquet, and inventoried and put away the equipment, consider giving your team and staff the month of December off and forget about football for a few weeks. Once the new year rolls around and school is back in session, however, your football program should be back in high gear with your off-season activities. Championships are won from January to June…not necessarily from September to November. This adage is designed to reinforce to coaches and players that what they accomplish in the off-season has a direct effect on how successful they will be once the season starts.

#10: Off-Season Quarterback Meetings

Many states do not allow coaches to work with players on the field during the off-season. However, no reason exists that you can't "chalk talk" with your players, and the players who need the most time on the white board are your quarterbacks. Meet with your quarterbacks once a week before school during the off-season. Distribute a copy of your quarterback's manual and cover the material for the first few meetings, which should each last about 45 minutes. Mix in aspects of your offense as you discuss topics from the manual. The manual should be mostly about the "intangibles" of being a successful quarterback. The chalk talk period is for discussing such topics as how to read pass coverages, reading progressions in your pass patterns, and how to avoid a blitz. You should use game tape cut-ups to give examples of both good and bad decisions. The meetings can get pretty intense at times as you stress the importance of making good decisions on- and off-the-field. These meetings are great opportunities to assess the attitude and dedication of your quarterbacks.

If you are allowed to instruct your quarterbacks on the field during the off-season, meet twice a week to tutor them on quarterback mechanics and then throw the ball, throw the ball, throw the ball! An effective drill that teaches finding the open man is to play 2-on-1 and 3-on-2 against a secondary. Show the quarterback what the two primary pass patterns are and run them against air for several reps until the quarterback becomes comfortable with where his primary receivers are going to be. Then add just one defender and instruct him to either "jump" one receiver or the other. Your quarterback has to drop, read, and throw to the uncovered receiver. You must constantly harp on making good choices. At the next morning meeting, review what you learned on the field from the previous workout. A head coach and/or offensive coordinator cannot spend too much time working with his quarterbacks during the off-season. This time is when most "game knowledge" improvement occurs.

#11: Offensive Linemen Blocking Rules Meetings

Meetings with offensive linemen during the off-season are crucial. You should consider meeting individually with three or four of your offensive linemen twice a week during the off-season during their lunch period. These meetings will each take about 20 minutes to review different aspects of your offensive system.

Before you start talking about blocking rules, teach the linemen the concepts involved in your offense. You should talk about the different types of blocks each lineman has to use and help him to have a picture of what every play or series is designed to do against a defense. Then you can introduce his individual blocking rules. Refer to Figure 2-1 for a sample blocks list. A unique tip to help understand this concept is to use an old electric football game. Line up the players in your offensive formation on the game board, and put a defense up against them. Don't hit the button; simply use the figures to create a visual image for the player as to what happens as the play unfolds. For the visual learner, this approach is an excellent means of illustrating a point and is more realistic than just drawing X's and O's on a piece of paper.

Blocks List for #3 Tackle			
Plays to the Left		**Plays to the Right**	
Play	*Rule*	*Play*	*Rule*
19 rocket	Fire on LB	11 rocket	Zone pull to LB
29	Area: center field	21	Gap-down-LB
28	Area: cross field	22	Gap-down-LB
26 trap	Gap-LB	24 trap	First LB from 5 man
21 waggle	Pull-check	29 waggle	Gap-down-(reach) on
21 waggle solid	Pull-check	29 waggle solid	Gap-down-on
39 power	Fire step-LB	31 power	Gap-on-area
38	Fire step-LB	32	Gap-post-lead
37 X-X	Fire step-area	33 X-X	Gap-lead-on
36 counter	Pull; trap first man past 5	34 counter	LB

Figure 2-1. Sample blocks list

#12: Coaches' Clinics

One of the main tenets of any head coach must be to challenge each of your assistant coaches to strive to become a "student of the game." Particularly for the young coach who is aspiring to be a coordinator or head coach one day, it is critical for him to gain as much knowledge of the game as possible during the off-season. You should always take one trip to a clinic together as a staff, but also encourage aspiring coaches to attend clinics on their own. Successful coaches must always be looking to gain a wider base of expertise.

One *little thing* that you should do is to arrange to meet with another high school staff in your state. Mega clinics are excellent, but the chance to meet for a day or more with another staff one-on-one is extremely beneficial. Questions can be more easily posed and only subjects that you want to discuss are covered. Be sure to record every session. You can also share copies of the recordings with any coach who wants one. Encourage every coach to have his own library of coaching clinic tapes (refer to #13: Coaching Videos and DVDs Library).

#13: Coaching Videos and DVDs Library

It is extremely important to have your own video library of coaching clinics. Several production companies make coaching videos. If you order a video that does not meet your needs, you can trade it in for another, as these companies all have return policies. You can buy five or six videos for the price of attending one clinic and never have to leave home.

Every coach needs to have a video library at his house of subjects that deal with his coaching area. You should also have a central library in the coach's office at the stadium. If a coach wants a particular video, he can check it out just like he would from the public library. Most of the professionally-produced videos cannot be copied legally, however, so the assistant can't make his own copy, but the videos are available to be taken home and viewed.

#14: Off-Season Weight Room

One of the keys to success for any high school football program is an off-season weight-lifting program. Even if you have to start from scratch with just a handful of potential players, you must open that weight room and get a program started. If you need some expertise in weight-training, you can contact the nearest college football program and ask to meet with their strength and conditioning coach. Find out what he does and ask him to show you what he'd recommend for a high school program. You can also contact Bigger Faster Stronger in Utah. Not everyone likes BFS's program but it is well-organized and built around helping high school athletes improve through strength and speed training. BFS has a tremendous array of resources available.

Once you have developed your program, you have to get athletes in the weight room, which can be challenging if weightlifting has never been emphasized at your school. Meet with the returning underclassmen as soon as possible and let them know what you will be starting. Talk to athletes in the halls and invite newcomers out to your weight program. Of course, once you get them in the weight program you have to motivate them to *stay* in the program. A lot of teens seem to think that if they lift for just a few weeks they will look like Mr. Universe. They have no concept of committing to six months of lifting to just begin to get stronger and faster.

Keep the athletes interested by first emphasizing the competitive aspect. Max out once a month, then post the top lifters in each weight class on the bulletin board and announce their names on the school PA system. Put the results in the local paper. Have a push-up contest once a week. Have a one-on-one tug-of-war contest. Have them compete in a Sumo-type wrestling tournament. Time them in the 40-yard dash once a month and post the scores. Then, for motivation, be sure that the winners get a tangible reward. Find something to reward effort and achievement, such as printed t-shirts, or some free food gift certificates from the local fast food restaurant.

It is also critical to make a big deal over the players who have great attendance. You have to find ways to motivate them to keep coming back. Monthly attendance awards are a means of encouraging attendance. Remember, if you want a behavior repeated, reward it.

#15: Players' Volunteer Hours

More and more coaches are making volunteer hours a mandatory part of their players' football experience. Beau LeBore, the head coach at Woodbury High School in Minnesota, requires his players to accumulate a specific number of hours of volunteer service in the community as part of the requirement to participate in football. He also offers a "W@YS" Award (Woodbury at Your Service) to the young men who accumulate at least 20 documented hours of service during the school year and meet all participation requirements of the football team. The service requirement is a tremendous opportunity to teach a practical life lesson in giving back to the community. Many young people are never exposed to the concept that giving is receiving. Coach LeBore wants the volunteer experience to shape who his players will become as adults. His aim is to teach them that the satisfaction lies in service to others—with nothing in return but knowing that they did something to help their fellow man.

This effort can be a team project or a player can work alone, but a certain number of hours need to be documented and accumulated over the school year. One example of a simple team volunteer project is cleaning up the football stadium the day after the school's graduation ceremony is held there. Another annual volunteer project can be to have your team meet on a Saturday morning in May and clean up the fields. Then a group could fertilize while another fills in holes with top soil. You can tell them, "It's your field. You get to help take care of it."

Also offer your team's volunteer services to community organizations, which can always use the help of 25 to 50 strong teenagers. For example, on his last day of pre-season camp, Coach LeBore takes his team to the local food bank and they stock shelves at the warehouse.

#16: Off-Season Monthly Staff Meetings

It is important during the off-season to keep in contact with your staff. A lot of assistant coaches work outside the school. Thus, it is not as easy to see those individuals on a regular basis. It is recommended that your staff meet once right after Christmas to plan your off-season strength- and speed-training program and see who can volunteer time to help in the weight room. It is probably not necessary to meet again as a staff until April. Then, arrange to meet with your staff once a month until the end of school, which should give you at least three monthly off-season staff meetings.

The first meeting is an overview of what you are planning on offense for the fall. The next meeting should focus on defense. The last meeting is similar to the January meeting in that you present your summer weight program and talk about pre-season plans. These meetings are particularly important if you have brought new coaches to your staff since the end of the past season. You should consider holding these meetings at your house, which allows you to extend some hospitality and welcome everyone in a more relaxed environment than meeting at school.

Note: It is strongly recommended that any time that you are meeting with your staff for a professional event that no alcoholic beverages be served. Though these off-season monthly meetings are set in a more relaxed atmosphere, it is still school business. You are representing your school, your principal, your athletic director, and yourself. Your staff is constantly evaluating you based on the "messages" you send—whether you do it consciously or unconsciously. Therefore, be sure you are sending the message you want. The type of beverages you serve at a staff get-together sends a huge message as to what your values and standards are.

#17: Off-Season Player Goal-Planning/Self-Evaluation Meetings

During February and March of every off-season, you should meet individually with each veteran player to discuss his team and personal goals for the next season and review a self-evaluation sheet (Figure 2-2) and a goal-planning sheet (Figure 2-3) that he has completed for you. The initial meeting is to explain what the exercise is all about and how he is to complete the information. Then make an appointment when it is convenient for the player (before school, during lunch or study hall, or after school) to meet with you for a 30-minute review.

The self-evaluation form gives you an opportunity to see what the players think of their own skill level. This experience is always enlightening, as many high school players vastly overestimate their ability level and some real tact is required on your part to bring them to a more realistic perspective of themselves. Ask them if they want to see what number you, as their coach, would circle for a particular trait (typically, most of them do want to know). This discussion opens the door to talk about how you evaluate them, and, more importantly, what areas they need to improve upon—whether it's speed, attitude, or strength. The sessions are always informative and really help set the tone for the off-season.

The next step is to discuss the goals the players listed for the upcoming season on the goal-planning sheet. Also talk with the players about their family and their interests, based on the information they provided on the form. One of the most revealing questions, and one that a number of the players struggle with, is "where do you see yourself 10 years from now?" Always ask them to be sure to give you the steps they feel they have to take to achieve any goal. Getting the kids to open up and share things of a personal nature is critical to building a strong rapport with them. As their football coach, you want them to know that you hold them in high regard as people and not just as players. Graduating seniors will often remark about how special this "talk" is to them.

Self-Evaluation

Rate yourself from 1 (lowest) to 5 (highest) on each of the following traits

Ability

Division 1	Small college	All-district	Starter	Make team
5	4	3	2	1

Speed

Outstanding	Very good	Good	Average	Poor
5	4	3	2	1

Movement (ability to change direction quickly)

Exceptional	Very good	Good	Average	Poor
5	4	3	2	1

Awareness and Intelligence (making good decisions on the field)

Great instincts	Tell me once	Learn quickly	Learn with reps	Hard to teach
5	4	3	2	1

Toughness (mental and physical)

Real hitter	Reckless	Good hitter	Fair hitter	Poor hitter
5	4	3	2	1

Strength

Exceptional	Very good	Good	Average	Poor
5	4	3	2	1

Durability

Always at practice	Plays hurt	Recovers fast	Slow recovery	Injury prone
5	4	3	2	1

Character (honesty & reliability)

Outstanding	Good citizen	Average citizen	Questionable	Poor
5	4	3	2	1

Persistence

Never gives up	Keeps trying	Pessimistic	Gives up easily	Quitter
5	4	3	2	1

Academics

Desire to excel	Work hard	Study when needed	Do minimum	Lack interest
5	4	3	2	1

Total points _____   **By coach** _____   **Date** _____

Strengths:

Areas to improve:

Figure 2-2. Self-Evaluation Sheet

Goal-Planning Sheet

Name _____ Date _____

Address _____ Phone _____

Parent(s) name _____

Siblings' name(s) _____

Favorite class in school _____

Least favorite class _____

How long have you played organized team football? _____

Names of teams _____

What are your goals for our team next season?
-
-
-

What will it take to achieve those goals?

What are your individual goals for yourself next season?
-
-
-

What will it take on your part to achieve those goals?

Where do you see yourself 10 years from now?

Figure 2-3. Goal-Planning Sheet

#18: Kicker Tryouts

It is critically important to learn early in your career as a head coach that you should have a quality snapper and place kicker if you want to have a successful football program. Ask your school's soccer coach if he can recommend some of his players who he thinks could kick a football as well as they boot a soccer ball.

It may be necessary to place an ad in your school newspaper and post bulletins around the school that you are going to have football team place-kicking tryouts and anyone interested in seeing if he can make the varsity football team as a kicker should report to the stadium the following week. At the tryouts, let them stretch and then give a short clinic on how to line up, approach, and kick a football. Throw out a bag of balls, put one on a tee (no holder at first) and let one player at a time kick six balls. It will be obvious after a couple of rounds who is talented enough to possibly help the team. Chart every kick as to good or no good and give them "style" points. Then invite the top two kickers to return the next day for a kick-off. Bring a holder out, have him set the ball on the block (no snap), and begin the competition. After three rounds of 12 balls, it should be obvious who the better kicker is. Congratulate both of the athletes, announce the winner, and let him know that he has made the varsity football team. You can also ask the second player to join you. He is probably interested in being part of your team also since he has invested time and effort into competing for a position. You then have all summer to let your snapper, holder, and kickers go off on their own and kick a bag of balls while you attend to weight lifting.

Explain to your soccer-team kickers that they are as much a part of your team as any other player. Do not allow them to get out of condition and tell them that they are expected to be at every practice. It is okay to allow them to leave early after they complete their kicking workout and do the team conditioning for the day. It is advisable to discourage them from playing on any soccer team during football. However, rules could prohibit you from keeping them from playing soccer if they or their parents choose to let them play during football season. It is important to have them practice tackling fundamentals on the one-man tackling stick since one of them will have to kick off, which means that your kicker may have to make a tackle in the game and you want him well versed in the fundamentals of making a safe, fundamental tackle. Most soccer players are very good athletes and can help in your kickoff coverage if you work with them.

#22: Leader Board

Once the superstars competition is completed, calculate the players' scores. If a player breaks a record in his weight class or breaks a school record for that event, place his name on a huge white board that hangs in your weight room. Leave his name on the board until his record is broken. The leader board is a real source of pride and you will see former players come in years later to show their son their name on the leader board.

You should also have several ways to recognize those players who exhibit tremendous strength in the individual lifts in the weight program. Your emphasis should be on the bench, power cleans, squats, and push jerk as your core lifts. If a player lifts, for example, 300 or more pounds, his name is engraved on the "300 pound bench club" plaque that hangs in the weight room. The leader boards are great motivators and a means of getting recognition for your players. Figure 3-1 provides a sample superstars leaders list.

Superstars Record Breakers			
Name	Weight Class	Record	Event
C. Tyson	(141-155)	4.10	Agility run
B. Barnson	(141-155)	106	Abs
F. Washington	(156-170)	275	Bench press
F. Washington	(156-170)	270	Power cleans
M. Cheeks	(156-170)	116	Abs
S. Simmons	(156-170)	4.21	Agility run
S. Simmons	(156-170)	235	Push press
J. Conyers	(171-185)	42.2	Dot drill
J. Conyers	(171-185)	114	Abs
R. Hill	(171-185)	4.21	Agility run
D. Ferguson	(186-200)	105	Abs
M. Cannella	(216-230)	*111	Abs
J. Hollaway	(231 plus)	104	Abs
J. Hollaway	(231 plus)	4.43	Agility run
J. Hollaway	(231 plus)	280	Power cleans

*School record

Figure 3-1. Sample superstars leaders list

#23: 1,000 Pound Club

Setting goals is a key to motivation. Without a target to shoot at, the player doesn't really know why he is working so hard. The culmination of your off-season weight-lifting program each year is your superstars competition. During superstars, you should have your max outs in your four main lifts: bench, power clean, squat, and push press. Make the days that you have your "lift-offs" a time of great anticipation and excitement. The goal for the players is to accumulate a total of at least 1,000 pounds in the four lifts. If they achieve this goal, they are inducted into the 1,000 Pound Club and are given a special 1,000 Pound Club t-shirt. Conduct a presentation ceremony as part of your player/parent orientation meeting so the weightlifters can be recognized in front of the parents.

#24: 1,200 Pound Club

The ultimate in achievement in your weightlifting program is to be inducted into the 1,200 Pound Club. This level separates the really strong kids from the good lifters. To accumulate 1,200 total pounds in your four core lifts is a remarkable achievement; but one that you want all of your athletes to strive for. Because of this accomplishment, make induction into the 1,200 Pound Club a special *little thing*. Not only will the players who achieve this goal receive a t-shirt—their t-shirt should have a special multi-colored design so it really stands out. Every player who earns 1,200 Pound Club status should also receive a plaque to take home with him. Mount a special plaque on the wall in your weight room to recognize those weightlifters who achieved 1,200 Pound Club status. The names of all 1,200 Pound Club members and the year they accomplish their goal are etched in an individual plate on the plaque so that anyone who comes in your weight room can see it.

#25: Weightlifting Hall of Fame

One of the most important aspects of an effective weight program is to get kids in the weight room, but, more importantly, to *keep* them in the program over a three- to four-year period. Recruiting players as young as eighth grade is the key to making this goal happen. To motivate players to get started in your strength program early in their career, develop a weightlifting hall of fame. The requirements for induction into your hall of fame should fall along the guidelines of: one, a player must lift year-round in your program at school for a minimum of three years; two, he must achieve at least 1,000 Pound Club status; and three, he must exhibit a positive attitude and strong work ethic and be a leader in the weight room. This status is all based on the strength and conditioning coach's judgment.

Place a huge plaque on a wall in your weight room with the names engraved of all of the players who have been inducted into your weightlifting hall of fame, as well as the year they are inducted. You should also present each individual player with a plaque at your season-ending team banquet and really play it up that his achievement is outstanding. All athletes enjoy getting recognized in front of their peers, and if young players see another child get an award in front of the parents, it is very motivating.

This award can be achieved by any player on the team, but almost always goes to seniors who have completed their three years minimum in a weight program. It isn't a competitive award—any player from the perennial back-up offensive lineman to the all-state running back is capable of achieving hall of fame status. Also, when you get that eighth-grader in your program for the first time, you can point to the weightlifting hall of fame plaque on the wall and tell him, "That can be *you* some day—*if* you stick it out in here over the next four years."

#26: Slogan for Team T-Shirt

A great way to highlight your team philosophy is to choose a slogan for the upcoming season and have it screen-printed on the back of your team t-shirt. It is important to get the players involved in the selection process so they can feel like they are investing in their football program. Prepare a list of four or five slogans that you think would be appropriate for what your team is focusing on for the upcoming season and submit that list to a group of veteran players or seniors for their recommendation. Or, if you have a slogan that you feel is the single most important factor in your upcoming run for a championship season, present only that idea and "sell" it to the veterans. The players usually wear their team t-shirt everywhere, including under their pads. As a result, that slogan is out there being seen all the time.

#27: Wearing Game Jerseys to School on Game Day

Athletes wearing their game jerseys to school on game day is a tradition that many schools adopt. It is a way to gain some recognition for your players around school. Emphasize to your players that this jersey is a source of team pride and wearing it carries a huge amount of responsibility. With the jersey on their back, people will know that they play for your school and will be watching them. These athletes have a higher standard to uphold than the rest of the student body. Wearing the jersey is a privilege and an honor—something that doesn't put them above the rest of the student body, but sets them apart. They work hard to earn it and they should wear it with pride. Some coaches even require their players to wear a collared shirt and tie under the jersey. Your players need to wear their jerseys as a badge of honor.

#28: Helmet Stickers

Helmet stickers are a tremendous source of motivation. Every week, give out the following stickers:

- Star = all team members for a win
- Football = players of the week:
  - ✓ Offense
  - ✓ Defense
  - ✓ Special teams
  - ✓ Scout team (offense and defense)
- Skull and crossbones = special teams objectives met
- O = offensive team objectives met
- D = defensive team objectives met
- Pride = outstanding job/improvement in academics or service to school

Because the players are being rewarded for something good that they did, they are motivated to repeat it. Reward the behavior that you want to see and you will see it show up more often on the field. Offensive, defensive, and kicking teams can earn their sticker for achieving their game objectives. Distribute game balls to the outstanding performers—not a real football, but a helmet sticker in the shape of a football. You should not only recognize the outstanding offensive and defensive performers, but you should also recognize and reward the kicking game player of the week and the scout team players of the week, which is an opportunity to recognize a couple of reserves or underclassmen for great work on the scout teams in practice.

#29: "Big Play" Helmet Stickers

Although you should always emphasize "team," you also need to reward individuals who exhibit great effort. When a player goes "above and beyond" during a game, you should recognize that great effort with a sticker related to your team mascot (e.g., a big cat paw). Big hits are a separate category (refer to #30: "Big Hit" Helmet Stickers). Big plays are determined by the effort put forth. For example, that defensive tackle who gets knocked down at the line but gets up and hustles downfield 35 yards to get in on the tackle—that effort is a big play. A running back who runs over or through the first tackler and struggles for a key first down, a receiver who lays out and makes a great catch (a "pro" catch), a defensive end who beats the offensive lineman in front of him and tackles the ballcarrier for a loss, and a player who runs a great pursuit angle and saves a touchdown because of his hustle are all examples of the type of great effort that should be rewarded, in hopes of having that effort repeated by all of the players. These big plays are the ones to look for when you make the highlight video on Sunday to show to the team on Thursday. Recognize the players and then reward them with a helmet sticker for going above and beyond to make a big play for your team.

#30: "Big Hit" Helmet Stickers

If you want more aggressive play on the field, then you need to reward it when you see it. If a big hit occurs in practice, blow the whistle and call all the players up around you. Always carry a couple of hammer (i.e., "big hit") helmet stickers. Ask the player who just made the big hit in practice for his helmet, pull out a sticker, and slap it on. The kids will go wild.

When you show the highlight video to the team on Thursday, stop the projector after a big hit and ask the player to bring his helmet up to you. If you slap the hammer sticker on his helmet, a big round of applause will break out. These actions are *little things* that players pick up on and get excited about.

Big hits don't have to be just tackles. An offensive lineman who gets a down block that wipes out a defensive lineman, a tight end downfield who gets a peel-back block at the sideline, or a wide receiver who gets a big hit on a crack-back block should all be recognized for a big hit. Players on special teams covering kicks can also get a "big hit" sticker. The hit has to be clean and you never want to recognize cheap shots, but when a player makes that extra effort to really lead with his pads and unload on an opponent fair and square, you want it to be recognized. You will find your hammer sticker output will expand exponentially after the first year you begin handing out "big hit" awards.

#31: "Lay the Wood!" Big Block Award

It is common knowledge that the players on a football team who labor the hardest and get the least recognition are the offensive linemen. A great idea to get these unsung heroes some well-deserved attention is to purchase a big block of wood (an old 2x4 about 18 inches long) and paint it with your school colors. The offensive lineman who, in the coach's estimation, plays the best and works the hardest in practice is presented with the Lay the Wood! Big Block Award for the outstanding offensive lineman of the week. The award winner then autographs the block of wood. The following week, when a new lineman earns the award, it is handed off to him and he autographs it. Hopefully, by the end of the season a majority of the linemen will win the award.

#32: Wall of Fame

Many NFL teams prominently display the names of their former outstanding players in their stadiums. For example, the Dallas Cowboys have a ring of honor on the upper deck façade. You can do something similar in your locker room by creating a "wall of fame" to recognize your former players who have been honored with all-district, all-region, all-state, or all-American honors. At the end of each season, add the names of your players who earned one of these honors.

When you start this project, in order to have the names of all honored players in the history of your school, you need to find the names of those players who made all-district or better in the past. Paint one row of cinder blocks one school color and the row right above it your other school color. Then, with the opposite color paint, print the names in calligraphy of those players from the past on the row of blocks and include the year that they earned the honor beside their name. Print two names on one block and move to the next block to the right and paint two more names. As the years go by, you will complete a ring around the locker room with your honored players' names and may even have to start back at the beginning to inscribe more names. You will find that you will have your young players tell you that, "before I graduate Coach, I'm going to get my name up there on the wall." The wall of fame is a tremendous source of pride and a great way to chronicle the history of outstanding players that your school's program has produced.

#33: Team Awards

Present your team awards for the season at the end-of-year team banquet. When voting, you might consider doing things a little differently: first, every player and coach has one equal vote; and second, include overall team awards, as well as individual position awards. This list should include Offensive Lineman of the Year, Offensive Back of the Year, Receiver of the Year, Defensive Lineman of the Year, Linebacker of the Year, and Defensive Back of the Year. It is critical to also present a Special Teams Player of the Year, Scout Team Player of the Year, Rookie of the Year, Outstanding Leadership Award, and a Scholar/Athlete of the Year (highest GPA on the team) to your players. These athletes are those "unsung" players who also deserve credit and recognition for the fine job they perform all season. At this point, you can vote for and present the Outstanding Offensive Player of the Year, Outstanding Defensive Player of the Year, and, finally, your Most Outstanding Player awards. With 45 to 60 players and so many different skills emphasized on a football team, it is necessary to recognize the best at each position, which means that a lot of players are recognized for outstanding achievement. By allowing players and coaches to have one vote each, the question of a coach playing favorites will be averted. Also, by having so many awards, the chance of more players being recognized increases.

Only those players who earn their letters should be given their chenille and certificate. Also, players must achieve standards, which are set and presented in the player policy sheets, to win their varsity letter. Those players who don't letter can receive a certificate of participation.

#34: Season Goal Poster

It is important to meet with your seniors in June each year to discuss team goals for the upcoming season. You can have a cookout or pizza and then talk about goals. Once the seniors have shared what they think your goals should be, you should take their recommendations and compose a final list of what you feel are realistic/optimistic goals for your season. Make a poster of the goals on a large piece of poster board, have it laminated, and attach it to the locker room wall (refer to Figure 3-2 for a sample poster). Be sure to refer to it frequently just to remind the players what they are working toward.

Before you take the field for your very first pre-season practice, talk to your players and staff about the goals on the chart and reinforce that these goals are the reasons your team is going out on that practice field that day and every day until you finish your season.

Note: Most of your team goals should deal with performance and team issues, not winning games or championships. Become a believer in emphasizing to your staff and players that execution and effort will bring you long-term success. If you take care of the *little things* along the way, it will spell victory on Friday night.

Season Goals

- Maximize practice (earn every penny every day of pre-season practice).
- Maintain strong team unity throughout the season (do things together and encourage each other).
- Do not allow any negativity in the locker room, on the practice field, or on the sideline during games (15 push-ups penalty).
- Accept responsibility for your mistakes (no excuses).
- Have an excellent pre-season in preparation for the regular season.
- Execute, play with enthusiasm, and encourage each other during scrimmages.
- Be consistently superior throughout the season (earn your team's sticker every week).
- Play like champions (come back to win at least one game in the fourth quarter).
- Exhibit sportsmanship throughout the week and every game (no ejections).
- Respect team policies and strive to be a better man when the season is over than you were when it started (no punishment periods for off-the-field problems in school or in the community).
- Make your opponent fear you—and respect you (skull hits).
- Be in better condition than anyone on our schedule (physically dominate in the fourth quarter).
- Win our opener.
- Keep the cup.
- Improve every week during the season (keep drive-batting average going up).
- Regain the respect of our opponents.
- Play in December (regional champions).
- Get a ring! (state champions)

Figure 3-2. Sample goal poster

#35: Schedule Poster

During the week leading up to pre-season practice, hang a laminated poster on a wall in the front of your locker room that has your upcoming game schedule on it (refer to Figure 3-3 for a sample poster). For example, when Gary Barnett was at Colorado, he highlighted in red the game that was the key to having a championship season. Barnett stated that they knew at Colorado that they had to beat Nebraska if they ever wanted to win a Big 12 championship. Every year he highlighted Nebraska in red on the poster. Accordingly, everyone pointed to that game as *the* game of the year.

Select the game that you feel is the one team that you need to point to more than any other on your schedule. It may be your cross-town rival or it may be the team that has won in your league more than any other team. After you print out all the names of the teams you'll be playing, highlight that one particular team's name. When you attach it to the locker room wall, that highlighted team will really stand out and your kids will point toward that game as practice begins. Arrange the games in ascending order on the poster to give the appearance that your team is climbing a ladder as they see each game come up. You can call it the "ladder of success."

Figure 3-3. Sample schedule poster

#36: Signs in the Locker Room

Post motivational signs around the locker room and weight room to plant seeds of a positive mind-set in your players. The key is to repeatedly bring up motivational messages to your players and challenge them to adopt whatever the saying on the sign refers to. Find slogans that represent those core values that you want your program to stand for and get those signs up on the walls. Written messages have a tremendous impact on young people.

#37: "No Excuses" Sign

Ask a local sign-making company to print up a 12 x 12 inch sign that reads "no excuses," which you can attach to the wall just above the main entrance/exit to your locker room. Tell each player to touch the sign every time he leaves the locker room to remind him that you do not want whiners—you do not want players who make alibis for making mistakes. Touching the sign every time the players leave the locker room is a reminder that *if* they give you 100 percent effort, no one is going to get on them if they mess up. Explain to the players that what you want from them is effort—*not* excuses. This sign is an effective motivator because you will be constantly reminding them throughout the year about the importance of not pointing fingers and not making excuses if a coach corrects you.

A no-excuses sign is particularly significant when another off-season weight-lifting program begins and you have a new group of rookies. It's amusing to watch them jump up and touch the sign along with the veterans as they leave the locker room, knowing that they have no idea as to why they are touching the sign. After a week or so, during a team meeting before weight training begins, talk to them about what the sign means and why everyone touches it. It is even more effective to ask a veteran to explain it in front of everyone. When new players hear veterans talking about the *little things* that make your program special to them, the rookies really take notice and quickly assimilate these things into their behavior.

#38: "Expect to Win" Sign

One of the principles of learning that a coach needs to be cognizant of is that if you want to change someone's behavior, you first have to change his thinking. If you are running a football program that has not been very successful, a "loser's attitude" may grip your team and you need to turn that mind-set around. Talk to your players and coaches about being successful and be careful to be very positive and encouraging while you are instructing and correcting. You can tell by the look on the players' faces when you fall behind on the scoreboard that you are going to lose.

Place a sign that reads "expect to win" on the wall beside the exit door so that the players can see it every day when they leave the locker room. Change starts in a person's mind, the way a person thinks determines the way he feels, and the way a person feels influences the way he will act. Talk to your players about the need to go out on the field on Friday night and *expect* to win. Remind them that they work hard, they are good athletes, and they know their assignments. It is just a matter of *believing* that they are going to win. Don't worry about the scoreboard—whether you are ahead or behind, just keep *expecting* to win. The sign will have a tremendous effect on the mental toughness that your players develop and maintain over the years.

4

Pre-Season Activities

Those few weeks that your state association gives you to prepare your team for your opening game and the subsequent fall schedule are a critical time in your preparation. While everything in the off-season points toward this pre-season period, when your practices start, everything changes—mentally and physically. The better organized you are as the head coach, the smoother things will run. This period is the first time that you will have everyone together who is vying for a spot on your roster.

A number of critically important *little things* exist that you must have in place in order for your coaches and players to be properly prepared for your season to begin. If you flounder in this final phase before the lights come on that first Friday, you are setting up your whole program for potential failure.

#39: Summer Planning

Lay out your installation schedule in June or July before practice starts as the staff needs to decide which plays/series will be a part of your offense. Then determine on a day-by-day basis when each play will be installed during pre-season practice. It is good to have a benchmark in terms of knowing when you want to install a certain number of plays. For example, you should have your base offensive series installed by your first scrimmage. Then a second benchmark is set for the number of plays you want to have installed by your second scrimmage. It is best to have most of your offense installed by the second scrimmage so you can just review after that point until you get to the first game. Therefore, it is important to have almost all of your core offense installed and reviewed by your final pre-season tune-up. Every couple of weeks into the regular season, you can introduce a new play to work on.

A rule of thumb everyone should follow is: practice a play for two weeks before you use it in a game. Once you have your installation schedule laid out on a daily basis, you can begin to formulate your pre-season daily practices (refer to sample schedules in Figures 4-1 and 4-2). Plan to have every individual pre-season practice schedule laid out, copied, printed up in packet-form, and presented to your staff at your pre-season staff meetings that occur the week before August practice begins.

Daily Offensive Installation Schedule

Thursday, August 3rd
Formations: 100/900 and strong; 400/600
Motion: fly
Audible: none
Shifts: flip-to
Run: 121/929; fly 621/fly 429; flip-to 121/929
Pass: 121/929 waggle; fly 621/fly 429 waggle

Friday, August 4th
Formations: review
Motion: review
Audible: review
Run: 124/926 trap; fly 426 trap/fly 624 trap
Pass: 121/929 waggle solid

Saturday, August 5th
Formations: review
Motion: hawk
Audible: review
Run: review
Pass: 90 series—hawk 499/691; hawk 498/692; hawk 497/697; hawk 496/694

Monday, August 7th
Formations: strong
Motion: jet
Audibles: review
Shifts: none
Run: roll-to hawk 482/688 down; jet 481/689 QB keep
Pass: Jet 482/688 KP and hawk 482/688 KP tar heel

Tuesday, August 8th
Formations: review
Motion: review
Audibles: review
Shifts: roll-to (tight end trade)
Run: zap 487/683; roll-to 483/687; roll-to fly 489/681 down sweep
Pass: Fly 683/487 KP; zap 683/487 KP pipe; roll-to 683/487 bootleg

Wednesday, August 9th (Camp Day #1)
Formations: review/Kicking: pat and punt
Motion: review
Audibles: review

Figure 4-1. Sample daily practice installation schedule

Shifts: review
Run: review 80's
Pass: review KPs and bootleg

Thursday, August 10th (Camp Day #2)
Formations: review/Kicking: kickoff and kickoff return
Motion: review
Audibles: review
Shifts: review
Run: 132/938; zap/fly 434/636 counter
Pass: 132/938 bootleg and 50's passes—51/59 (buckeye); hawk 454/656 cruise; 52/58 TH; 53/57 pipe

Friday, August 11th (Camp Day #3)
Formations: review/Kicking: punt block
Motion: review
Audibles: review
Shifts: review
Run: 137/933 X-X
Pass: review

Saturday, August 12th
Intra-Squad Scrimmage

Monday, August 14th
Formation: shotgun spread right and left
Run: shotgun 32/38; 24/26 mouse; 83/87; 83/87 Jersey mouse
Pass: 60s; 32/38 Nike; 83/87 Nike

Tuesday, August 15th
Formations: review shotun spread
Motion: hawk (to trips)
Run: review
Pass: hawk 91/99 flanker screen; 63/67 cruise

Wednesday, August 16th
Review

Thursday, August 17th
Pre-Game
Picture Day

Figure 4-1. Sample daily practice installation schedule (cont.)

Friday, August 18th
Scrimmage

Monday, August 21st
Review

Tuesday, August 22nd
Review

Wednesday, August 23rd
Pre-Game

Thursday, August 24th
Benefit Game

Friday, August 25th
Varsity Cookout
Review

Saturday, August 26th
Pass: 70 Series

Monday, August 28th
Formation: heavy 400/600
Run: zap/hawk 41/49; hawk 448/642 truck
Pass: zap 641/449 wingback pass; heavy zap 449 split end screen to 1

Tuesday, August 29th
Review

Wednesday, August 30th
Review

Thursday, August 31st
Run: strong jet 431/639 pitch; zap 139 quick pitch

Friday, Sept. 1st
Review

Monday, Sept. 4th
Labor Day
Game Week!

Figure 4-1. Sample daily practice installation schedule (cont.)

Daily Practice Schedule

Date	Team	Times
Monday, Aug. 8	Varsity only	4:15-9:15 p.m.
Tuesday, Aug. 9	Varsity only	4:15-9:15 p.m.
Wednesday, Aug. 10	Varsity only	4:15-9:15 p.m.
Thursday, Aug. 11	Varsity	4:15-9:15 p.m.
	JV	4:15-8:15 p.m.
Friday, Aug. 12	Varsity	4:15-9:15 p.m.
	JV equipment issue	10 a.m.-noon
	JV	4:15-8:15 p.m.
Saturday, Aug. 13	*Donut sale*	7 a.m.
	Varsity and JV	8:25 a.m.-12:45 p.m.
Monday, Aug. 15	*Camp day #1*	
	Varsity	7 a.m.-4:30 p.m.
	JV	7 a.m.-12:30 p.m.
Tuesday, Aug. 16	JV	7 a.m.-12:30 p.m.
Wednesday, Aug. 17	JV	7 a.m.-12:30 p.m.
Thursday, Aug. 18	Varsity and JV	6 p.m.-9:30 p.m.
Friday, Aug. 19	*Picture day*	9 a.m.-11 a.m.
	Varsity scrimmage	4:10 p.m.
	JV	TBA
Monday, Aug. 22	Varsity and JV	4:45 p.m.-9:30 p.m.
Tuesday, Aug. 23	Varsity and JV	4:45 p.m.-9:30 p.m.
Wednesday, Aug. 24	Varsity and JV	6:25 p.m.-9:15 p.m.
Thursday, Aug. 25	Varsity benefit game	4:10 p.m.
	(followed by Midnight Gold Diggers*)	
	JV	TBA
Friday, Aug. 26	Varsity	4:15 p.m.-6:30 p.m.
	Varsity team picnic	7 p.m.-8 p.m.
	JV	*No practice
Monday, Aug. 29	Varsity and JV	3:55 p.m.-8:15 p.m.
Tuesday, Aug. 30	Varsity and JV	3:55 p.m.-8:15 p.m.
Wednesday, Aug. 31	Varsity and JV	3:55 p.m.-8:15 p.m.
Thursday, Sept. 1	Varsity and JV	3:55 p.m.-8 p.m.
Friday, Sept. 2	Varsity and JV	3.55 p.m.-5:30 p.m.
Monday, Sept. 5	*Game week!*	3:55 p.m.-7.40 p.m.
Tuesday, Sept. 6	School opens	

*Refer to #49: Midnight Gold Diggers.

Figure 4-2. Sample daily practice schedule

#40: Seniors' Summer Cookout/Goal Planning Meeting

The more a head coach can do to bring his seniors "into the fold," the better off he's going to be. Players know as their junior year is drawing to a close that within weeks *they* will be the senior leadership on the next team. In fact, you should begin to plant the seeds of this fact in their minds as soon as the off-season weight-lifting program begins. At this point, start calling those players "football seniors."

It is worth the time and effort to hold a cookout at your house for the seniors the week after school is out in June. Invite all of the senior veterans by giving them a printed invitation delivered by hand. Hold the cookout on a week night so that weekend plans won't keep anyone from attending. Give the players several weeks notice so that they can work it into their schedules. Make sure that your seniors know how important this gathering is to you and to the team and every effort must be made to attend.

After eating and enjoying some fellowship, conduct your goal-planning meeting. Talk about what the players' expectations are for the upcoming season. It's important to emphasize two things: one, the success of the team will rise and fall on the senior leadership that you get from them from the summer through the playoffs; and two, the seniors need to play the best ball of their careers as they close out their high school playing days. The more you can reinforce to them that it is their last go-round, the more impact it will have on them to really be prepared for a great senior season. Point out that, for many of them, it will probably be the last time they will play organized football in a team setting. They all believe that they will play college football, but it's important to let them know that this season is the last time that they will play for you and their high school team. Give them a chance to process this information and encourage the seniors to comment about what they are feeling at that moment. After each player has a chance to say what's on his mind, then set about the task of coming up with your season team goals. Figure 4-3 provides a sample leadership handbook for your senior players.

Football Senior Leadership Handbook

I have always believed that the leadership a team receives from its seniors is crucial to the success of its season. *You* have the ability to make this year special or just average by the leadership you provide this team.

Leadership for your football team began as soon as last season ended. It continues through the winter and spring weightlifting and sports that you participate in together. In the weight room, around school and everywhere you go, our seniors must show us the way. This little handbook is intended to offer you some ideas and advice in helping your teammates in hopes that the positive leadership traits that each of you has within will start to surface as we move toward the start of practice in August.

We will only go as far as *you* want us to go. We will be as successful as *you* want us to be! We need to pull together and make your senior year a season to remember. Are you willing to **rise to the challenge** and make our team the best this year?

Effective leadership is oriented toward *goals*. You must find ways to get other members of your team to work with you to reach the team goals. Remember: They are not just the coach's goals—they are *your* goals. Someone who can gather loyal followers through the use of a nice personality, but is not effective in directing those followers (teammates) to achieve anything, is *not* a successful leader. We need you to pull us up to a higher level and make us a force to be dealt with. Leadership is not a personal characteristic but rather a dynamic process that works toward goal achievement.

We need you to come forward and set the example that you would like to see your team follow. You need to remember the great feelings when we win games. You also need to remember how lousy and empty it feels to deal with defeat. You must use these feelings to ignite a "fire" in your teammates. You must combine your effort and execution with theirs to make a difference.

You must use the memories of last season, the examples of seniors from your underclassman years, and your own knowledge of what it will take to be successful to get others to follow you. Then *you* must set the example of how you want others to act. *"Do right"* is an attitude and you must set the example. Remember: this is your last season. You will make your memories—make them great ones.

Figure 4-3. Sample senior leadership handbook

Hold the Rope

I'd like you to consider the following story as you decide if it's *worth* the cost of leading us to a great season. The story is called "Hold the Rope."

Every year, a professional football team wins the world championship. Every year a college team wins the national championship. Every year a high school team wins the state championship. All of these teams have one thing in common. No matter how tough it got throughout their season, they did one thing—*they held the rope!*

What is *holding the rope?* Imagine that you are hanging from the edge of a cliff with a sheer drop of 500 feet below. The only thing between you and a fall to your death is a rope...with the person of *your* choice holding on at the top of the cliff. Who do you know who has the guts to pull you to safety? Who do you know who will let the rope burn their hands and not let go? How many teammates do you know who are going to withstand the burning pain and watch blood drip from their hands for *you*?

If you can think of two players, that is not good enough. Those two guys might not be around. The next time your team is together, look around and ask yourself, "Whom can I trust to hold the rope?" "Who is going to let their hands bleed for me?" When you can look at *every* member of your team and say to yourself that they *all* would hold the rope, then our team is destined to win a lot of football games. The team that holds the rope when the going gets tough is a *winning team*. When you are down by two touchdowns and thoroughly exhausted, yell at your teammates to "hold the rope; let it burn; but don't let go!"

Every year, there are winners and losers in every sport—the winners are the ones who held the rope. You do not have to be the most talented team on the field every week to win the game. If you play with poise, do what your coaches ask of you, and, most of all, *hold the rope*, you will be successful. No matter what sport you play, in order to win, you must have a commitment to the team. If you are supposed to run 20 40-yard dashes...don't cheat—give it your all. Once you start letting up at practice or start missing weight-lifting workouts, you've killed the team because you did not hold the rope.

With this in mind, let me pose one last question to you: how many of your teammates thought of *you* when I asked who they feel they can count on to hold their rope? It's something to think about.

Don't let your team down—you have to *hold* the rope!

Figure 4-3. Sample senior leadership handbook (cont.)

#41: 7-on-7 Summer Passing Tournaments

An activity that you should consider getting started in your area is a 7-on-7 touch-passing league against the schools in your city. Set up a league schedule where you meet one evening a week at one of the schools and play two 30-minute (running clock) touch-passing games. Your local officials' association may loan you one of their officials because it is good training for their rookies (then the officials have control of the games instead of the coaches).

Some schools offer 7-on-7 tournaments. An entry fee is charged, so it becomes a fundraiser for the host school. These tournaments are organized and competitive. Teams come from the host area as well as across the state on a Saturday and play all day. Every team that enters is guaranteed at least three games. Then the semi-finals begin and the four teams with the best record from the preliminaries play for the trophy. It's a great way to play a lot of games in one day, let one school handle all the administration, and not have to worry about organizing a weekly league schedule. Plus, as indicated, you can use it as a lucrative fundraising event.

You will find these tournaments to be very helpful. You can run your offensive passing game and let your defense work on different coverages and the games are a great opportunity to see younger players compete and get an idea of who can go get the ball when it's in the air. Perhaps one of the more important "messages" that these tournaments will send to your players is: "we will throw the ball."

It may be surprising, but basketball players or track athletes exist who would be interested in playing football for you *if* they knew they could line up at wideout and stay away from a lot of the contact. Many teams that are primarily running teams still participate in the games just to keep their players interested during the summer. There is so much competition from other sports for athletes' time that you must have some football-related activity during the summer that will draw your skilled players to the football field. The weight room sometimes isn't enough to get them off of the basketball court. Playing in some touch football games, though, may be the "carrot" that will get them out for your team.

#42: Pre-Season Scrimmage Selection

When you are first trying to establish your program, look for scrimmages that you feel you can be competitive in. If you are struggling to build your program, the last thing you need to do is to set up a pre-season scrimmage with a perennial state power. The old adage that, "if you want to be the best, you have to play the best" is not for programs that are trying to get off the ground. You are trying to instill confidence in your players. The fastest way to crush that confidence is to get taken apart early in your season. Find a team in a similar situation as yours—regardless of whether you are just establishing your program or you are a power in your league. Play like-quality teams.

Once you have built a winning tradition at your school, your attitude can change regarding who you want to scrimmage. Then, it becomes a challenge to find schools that can compete with you. Use your scrimmages as preparation for the long haul to the playoffs. Strong competition in the pre-season develops the confidence and perseverance it takes to get to the post-season.

#43: Player/Parent Orientation Meeting

It should be a requirement that you and your coaching staff meet with your players *and* their parents before your season begins. It is very important to establish lines of communication before your practices begin. You should have a number of speakers (in addition to yourself) to talk to the players and parents, including your trainer and team doctor who can talk about hydration, injury prevention, and the procedure to follow if a player is injured. Your athletic director should be asked to come and speak on sportsmanship, academic eligibility, and school athletic-department policies. The president of your booster club (if you have one) should be invited to speak and encourage parents to join the club and your strength and conditioning coach can hand out Superstars Competition awards (#21: Superstars Competition), 1,000 and 1,200 Pound Club Club t-shirts (#23: 1,000 Pound Club and #24: 1,200 Pound Club), and plaques.

Your main focus, however, must be on reviewing the player policy sheet(s) and discussing with parents their role in supporting their son and your program. Once the policies are reviewed, every player and his parent are required to sign the agreement page and turn it in to you before they leave. Covering those policies gives you the opportunity to establish and clarify exactly what your expectations are as far as how you will conduct yourself and how your program will be run.

Before the meeting starts, open up your "sportswear shop." You can sell team t-shirts, socks, baseball caps with your school logo, miniature helmets, sweatshirts, and shorts. Another popular item is the sale of used game jerseys. If you have jerseys that have been replaced by newer ones, you can sell the old ones at a reduced rate. Parents will buy them to wear to your games to exhibit the jersey number that their son wears. The players also like to buy them to wear around the community and to have keepsakes after they graduate. The one piece of apparel that you should strongly urge *every* player to buy is your team t-shirt, which is custom screened front and back for a particular season.

It is a long evening, but an important one. Let parents know that you are available to answer questions after the meeting is over and then open up the sportswear shop again.

#44: Paint the Practice Field

A freshly painted practice field to begin pre-season practice in August is a tremendous morale booster for everyone involved in your program. It also has practical value because your practice field is your classroom. You would not have a classroom without charts, resource books, or a white board to write assignments or notes upon. A practice field with lines gives you and your players a replica of the actual playing field: hash marks for your secondary and receivers; sidelines for running backs and receivers; and yard lines to give everyone a picture of where they will be on game night.

Your parents' maintenance or paint crew can help repaint the lines at least every two weeks (every week if you get rain). Keep two small spray-painting machines and cartons of spray cans in your storage facility and designate an assistant coach to be responsible for helping your student managers spray fresh lines before Monday's practice. It's a *little thing* that makes a big difference.

#45: Camp

Many teams conduct a pre-season camp during the first or second week of practice each year. Some places you can hold your camp are a college campus, a National Guard training facility, or a Boy Scout camp.

If these places are simply unfeasible because of lack of potential sites or your players cannot afford the cost of going away for five days, you can stay home and still conduct your camp. Figure 4-4 provides a sample daily camp schedule.

Bring your players in very early each morning (6:00 to 6:30 a.m.), practice from 7 a.m. until 5 p.m., and then send them home. Make sure that you eat lunch together, have plenty of time for meetings, and also set aside time for team-building exercises. The pre-season camp will really help you prepare for the upcoming season and also bring your team together as a unified group. The days are long, but the players will read about NFL training camps going on at the same time, and develop a sense of pride that they are going through the same thing as professional players.

You should plan to practice four times during the day, starting the morning with a conditioning/weight-lifting practice. The players are on the track at 7 a.m. to flex and run the conditioning for that day. If it is a lifting day, the linemen are running while the backs are lifting. When they are finished running, the backs come outside to condition and the linemen go to the weight room to lift. When that practice is completed, take a break, and have a meeting. During that meeting time, if there is a new play to install, draw it up for them. Head to the field at the conclusion of the meeting and have your second practice of the day. The concept is fundamentals on both sides of the ball. The morning is spent on individual and group work only.

Everyone then stays in the locker room and eats lunch together, which is followed by a "team-building" exercise. The athletes are inside and off of their feet for over an hour. That hour is one of the most important times you will spend with your players during the entire season. If team unity is a core value in your mission statement, then that hour of eating lunch together and then involving everyone in a team-building exercise will be extremely beneficial.

The next practice is all kicking game. When you go back out, the only equipment that your players wear will be their helmet and practice pants. You will be installing a new special team and reviewing the one you installed the previous day. With only helmets, this practice is obviously not live, but it should be full speed. By installing and focusing on your kicking game so early in pre-season practice, you are sending that all-important message to your players that our special teams must be "special."

The last practice of the day is teamwork (after a 15-minute break to get their full pads on). During this practice, you can go full contact at times to get an idea of who is aggressive and who can perform at full speed. It is important not to go live too much, as it is the fastest way to wear your players out and the risk of injury increases if you have full contact too often. Since the NCAA puts regulations on the college teams in terms of how much they can practice and how much full contact work they can have in the pre-season, it behooves the prudent high school coach to consider these factors when planning his pre-season camp practices.

Your practice should be done by 5 p.m. Remind your players that there is no conditioning period at this point (because you ran them hard to start the morning). Go inside and have your "penny-a-day" ceremony (refer to #48: Pre-Season Daily Penny Award), talk briefly to the team about how you felt the day went, and send them home. Remember to incorporate your "word of the week" in your talk. Meet with your coaches briefly to talk about personnel and make sure everyone is up to speed about the next day's schedule.

Football Camp Daily Schedule	
6:45 a.m.	Staff arrives
7:00 a.m.	Team arrives
7:25 a.m.	Team meeting
7:30-8:04 a.m.	Conditioning/weightlifting
8:05-8:14 a.m.	Dress/break
8:15-8:24 a.m.	To field
8:25-8:29 a.m.	Call 'em up
8:30-10:00 a.m.	Defensive positions/groups
10:00-10:04 a.m.	Water break
10:05-11:34 a.m.	Offensive positions/groups
11:35-12:34 p.m.	Lunch break
11:35-12:25 p.m.	JV team practice
12:30 p.m.	JV goes home
12:35-12:54 p.m.	Defense meeting
12:55-1:14 p.m.	Offense meeting
1:15-1:24 p.m.	To field
1:25-1:44 p.m.	Kicking game (install new team)
1:45-2:04 p.m.	Kicking game (review previous team)
2:05-2:14 p.m.	Water break/put pads on
2:15-3:04 p.m.	Defense team
3:05-3:09 p.m.	Water break
3:10-4:00 p.m.	Offense team
4:00 p.m.	Penny-a-day ceremony
	Staff meeting

Figure 4-4. Sample daily camp schedule

#46: Offensive Playbook

In some instances, the only people on your team who receive a playbook are coaches and quarterbacks. When players start asking for diagrams of plays to go with their rules sheet, it is time to start drawing up plays for them (refer to Figure 4-5 for a sample playsheet). A unique concept was found in an old University of Delaware offensive playbook. In the Blue Hen playbook, the rules were typed out and the offensive formation and defensive alignment were printed but there were no lines drawn on the play diagram itself. Apparently, Coach Harold R. "Tubby" Raymond and his staff had the players draw in the lines for their position during meetings.

When pre-season camp begins, have an offensive meeting in the morning after the first practice. Present a blank playbook page to your players each day as you introduce a new play. The sheet should have the rules for every position—your offensive formation is diagrammed and the defensive fronts you want to attack are already printed on it, but the diagram is blank. As you draw each assignment on your overhead projector or white board, the players draw the lines on their playsheet. Some players will only draw the line for their position, while other players will draw in everyone's assignment. The idea is to give them some "investment" into diagramming the play so that they *do* something and don't just have it spoon-fed to them. They then secure the playsheet in their notebook and have a visual reference for learning their assignments. As new plays are occasionally presented during the season, the same procedure should be followed and the player can place the new playsheet in his booklet.

A good playbook should also include your offensive and/or defensive philosophy. In your offensive book, you will want to include your base alignments, snap count, and other pertinent material in the front. It is important that each player knows that his playbook will be collected at the end of the season when he turns in his equipment and that he is responsible if he loses it.

Play Sheet With Blank Diagrams

Play 121

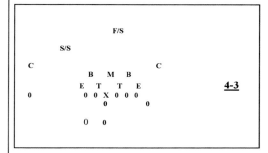

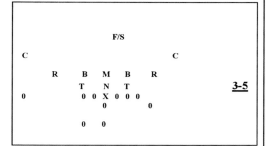

Split end: Stalk free safety

#7—Left tackle: Fire step; cross field and block cornerback.

#6—Left guard: Pull; turn up inside of #4's kickout block; wall off backside.

#5—Center: Step and protect playside A gap "on-away."

#4—Right guard: Pull; get depth; find wing's hip; kick out first man past wing's block.

#3—Right tackle: Gap; down; backer.

#2—Tight end: Gap; down; backer.

Quarterback: Reverse pivot; mesh with fullback; stay on midline. With back to line of scrimmage, hand off to halfback. Fake waggle at 9.

Halfback: Crossover step and run through fullback's toes. Receive handoff; read guard's blocks; make 90% cut into "tunnel."

Fullback: Dive for backside A gap. Fake trap and block whoever shows in a gap. "Faker/blocker."

Wingback: Step with inside foot; aim for tight end's hip; block first man inside.

Figure 4-5. Sample playsheet with blank diagrams

#47: Blocking Rules Tests

Players will not learn their play assignments unless they are motivated to do so. You should give your offensive linemen a rules test every day during the pre-season. It can be a short test of just three or four rules for the plays you have already installed, but the players should be expected to get all of the questions correct. For every wrong answer they should have to do some type of extra conditioning.

You will find, however, that some of your players are simply not motivated by this reprimand. What you will find to be effective is giving your backup more snaps in practice when he does better on his quiz than the starter does. This action motivates the second stringer to continue to work hard and learn his rules. Once your starter sees that there are consequences to not learning his rules (i.e., losing playing time or his starting position), he will also start doing much better on his rules tests.

Give every offensive player a rules sheet with the plays down the left hand side and the players' positions across the top. The offensive coordinator, along with the offensive line coach, must check this sheet before it is distributed to the players to be sure that every rule for every play is correct. Then the players will have a compilation of every rule they will need. The rules sheet can be distributed to veterans and key returnees during the off-season so they can begin to memorize their rules before practice even starts.

#48: Pre-Season Daily Penny Award

To emphasize how *every* day is critical as your team prepares for your opening game, find an old balancing scale like pharmacists used to use to weigh prescription drugs. Place 20 pennies (or the number of pre-season practices your association allows) on one side of the balancing scale to represent your first game opponent's 20 pre-season practices allotted by your state. Then at the end of each pre-season practice, drop a penny on "your" side of the scale. On the first day of practice, your side is going to be empty. Therefore, when you deposit those 20 pennies on the opponent's side, the scale is going to swing quickly to that side. When you drop your first penny, not much is going to happen. Watch the faces of your players as each day goes by. Remind them that every day is critical toward meeting your goal of being ready for your first game.

If your team practices hard and does it with enthusiasm, they "earn" their penny. If it is a bad day, the coaches can decide if the team should earn their penny that day. As the weeks go by, the players see that every penny is important. By the time you get to the day before your opener your scale may be starting to tilt back in your direction a little. When you drop that last penny on your side of the scale, the needle should swing to the middle and show that the scales are balanced. The kids will go wild! It shows them that they "paid the price" and they are now ready for that first opponent.

If they did not earn all of their pennies, then the scales will not be balanced and they will know that they have come up a little short in their preparation. Use that to your advantage and tell them that they will have to work extra hard in the game if they want to be victorious. If the "lost" penny day occurs during the second week of practice, you can come in the next day and make it a "two-penny day." The players will have to work exceptionally hard to make up for the penny they missed the day before. It's a tremendous motivator and keeps them focused during those rough days in August.

#49: Midnight Gold Diggers

On the night of your last pre-season scrimmage, have a solemn team ceremony to induct all players into the Gold Diggers Club. Tell all of the rookies ahead of time to bring a shovel to "dig gold" with. Remind all team members that they must bring a flashlight, pen, and paper. This ceremony is the closest you'll come to any type of "initiation." However, it is a very positive activity—one designed to build unity and pride. Your veterans will get excited because they've been through it. Your rookies will be in the dark until the ceremony is completed.

This ceremony occurs late at night after the scrimmage. March your team in silence from your locker room to a line designated as where your practice field begins. Speak to them in darkness and total silence about the importance of "G-O-L-D." Use the letters of "gold" to talk about four character traits that your players must exhibit as a team:

- **G** is for "goals." Have them write one team goal and one personal goal on a piece of paper.
- **O** is for "oneness." Talk about the importance of oneness or unity. Then tell them to write down the name of one member of your team (player or coach) that they know they can count on to be there for them when the times get tough. You should exhort them to tell that particular person that they wrote their name after the ceremony is completed.
- **L** is for "loyalty." Without loyalty, the whole team falls apart. Ask them to write down the name of one person that they are not getting along with at that time and that they will commit to improving the relationship.
- **D** is for "discipline." They must exhibit discipline to be successful. Have them write one thing that they need to improve their discipline in (i.e., doing homework, being on time, being respectful to their parents, or going to church).

Then, tell them that if they accept the challenge of living out what they wrote on that piece of paper to step forward with the rookies' shovels, dig a small hole, and bury their paper in the ground on that "jumping off" point at the edge of your practice field. Make sure it is a place that they will cross over every time they go to their practice field. You want it to be a constant reminder of the "gold" that is below their feet.

The rookies then step forward and start digging holes up and down the length of the line. If they are willing to follow through on what they wrote down, then once their piece of paper is buried, they are invited to step across the "gold mine" and meet the coaches. Give them a tiny "gold dot" punched out from a roll of helmet tape. Have a coach place their gold dot on the player's watch, wallet, or bill of their cap—anywhere where they will see that dot every day. It will remind them of the commitment they made to the team in those four areas. It's a very powerful moment.

Once your players and coaches cross the line on practice days, everyone is required to jog to the practice field because they should hustle everywhere they go. It helps set the tone for a good workday. Have a small sign (12 x 12) designed with a big gold dot and the letters G-O-L-D down one side placed on the locker room wall. You should also punch out numerous gold dots from the same helmet tape and place them in conspicuous spots around the locker room. The players will be constantly reminded of the importance of goals, oneness, loyalty, and discipline.

#50: Team/Family Picnic

A tradition that you should establish when you conclude your pre-season practices is to have a family picnic. A picnic is an opportunity to get the parents involved in your program by planning and implementing the event as well as just having all of the parents and siblings attend the function. It can be an informal, relaxed atmosphere where everyone enjoys the food and fellowship.

Announce the picnic at your orientation meeting but ask parents of veterans to start preparations when school lets out in June. A steering committee should be formed and the parents should handle all of the details. Players eat for free but parents and guests have to pay a nominal fee to partake, which helps buy hamburgers, hot dogs, and rolls. The rest of the food can be provided by the parents.

Consider holding the cookout in the stadium outside your locker room. You can use the tables from the school cafeteria. The parents should begin assembling around 4 p.m. for a 6:30 start, while your team is running through their last practice. While everyone is going through the food line, take the opportunity to meet players' parents and family. The picnic should be very informal so everyone enjoys their time together. When everyone is finished eating, use the amplifier system and talk to the families about your pre-season, the progress you've made, and your outlook for the season. It is important to be positive and optimistic no matter how many doubts you may have. Parents want to hear the things that are going well.

At this point, the coaches can recognize those players who have just completed an outstanding pre-season. Present certificates to the outstanding rookie, most improved, best hustler, and the player who exhibited great "teammanship." The teams' lieutenants can also be introduced.

The parents are usually great about cleaning up and allowing the coaching staff to head on home for some well-deserved time with their families. It is a great way to culminate pre-season practices and begin to focus on the opening game, which will be coming up in the following week.

#51: Team Lieutenants

Consider selecting lieutenants rather than captains on your team for two reasons: first, you will have more than one or two players getting the opportunity to learn leadership skills and take part in leading your team; and second, you run the risk of having a poor leader if you only have two captains and then you're stuck. With seven lieutenants, more players get leadership experience and if one lieutenant falters in his responsibility, you still have five or six to pick up the gauntlet and run with it.

The players and coaches nominate those players they believe will be your best leaders, but you should make the final selection, which must be based more on your observations of the particular player's leadership skills as opposed to who the players like. Too often, it turns into a popularity contest as far as who the players vote for, which is why you should make their vote merely a nomination. Count the nominations, take the nominees into consideration, and then determine who you want to be the team lieutenants. This nomination and selection process should take place the day before your first pre-season scrimmage. Figure 4-6 provides a sample lieutenants ballot.

When you have made your final selection, call each of them that night at home. Ask them point blank if they are willing to accept the responsibility of being a team leader, to emphasize to each of them how seriously you take the whole process. If they are willing to accept the standards of behavior that go with being a lieutenant, tell them that you are going to count on them to do it throughout the season.

On the next day (the day of your first pre-season scrimmage), buy lunch for the new cadre of lieutenants at a local restaurant. After eating, go over in detail what it means to be a lieutenant. Speak firmly and passionately about the importance of the lieutenants working closely with you—so closely, in fact, that, at times, you will call on them for advice before you even discuss something with your assistant coaches. You must establish a strong bond with these players. They will take care of a lot of things for you if they feel you trust and respect them.

You should have some form of "lieutenant's agreement" that each leader must sign after discussing what you expect from your team leaders. This agreement should state that each lieutenant understands his responsibilities as a leader and will abide by them. If, during the season, one of the lieutenants fails to abide by these tenets, he can and will be removed (demoted) from leadership.

Conduct a weekly meeting after practice each Monday to talk with the lieutenants. At this meeting, you want to get the pulse of the team. Distinguish if there are any concerns you need to know about and do a short lesson on various aspects of being a good leader. This step will help you know what is going on with the players and teaches the lieutenants that they are conduits between the coaches and players.

The coaches select "game captains" every Thursday. These four lieutenants then represent the team during the coin toss and are the spokesmen during conferences with the referee. The selection of a game captain is based on how well the lieutenant played in the previous game and how hard he practiced during that week. What you will discover is, as the season progresses, several of your lieutenants really begin to stand apart from the rest of the cadre and they will be selected week after week to be game captains. It is these two or three players who become recognized as your "real" captains. Time will prove to be the best test of leadership. Until those real leaders rise to the top, you will have team leaders in place who are developing strong skills and building a rapport with you.

Lieutenants Ballot

Name _____

Your job is to identify who you feel are the real *leaders* on your team. They are the players that you think will represent us the best on the field, in the locker room, in school, and around the community. It is a big responsibility, so please take your choices seriously. Not everyone can be a lieutenant. The players you nominate will be given a *lot* of weight in my final selection.

Circle the name or names of those players that you want to be considered for lieutenants. You may choose as few or as many on the list as you think deserve to be nominated. Be fair and honest in your selection. You may vote for yourself if you feel you deserve to be considered. I am looking for young men that you think have "committed to excellence," who are "big *team*…little *me*" players, who have a great work ethic, and who uphold our principle of team unity. That's who *you* should be looking for too. Remember: we are always looking for leaders. Someone can be "promoted" later in the season if he shows great leadership and the current leaders think he is worthy of being a lieutenant.

Rocky Rhodes	Jack Dempsey
Billy Joe Dibbs	Harold Stevens
Rob Whitener	Mickey Irvin
Steve Comfort	Roger Medlin
Ronnie Regan	Brian Burke

Figure 4-6. Sample lieutenants ballot

5

Practice and Game Preparation

A great coach is many things, but the best way to sum up all the qualities that an outstanding coach must possess is to say that he must be a master teacher. Knowledge of his subject, enthusiasm, organization of lesson presentation, and a genuine affection for his students are paramount to a successful classroom environment. The same holds true for the football coach. Practice time on the field is your laboratory. You are experimenting, instructing, and motivating your students. To be prepared for executing your game plan on Friday night, many long hours of preparation must take place on the practice field. The better prepared you are to implement effective principles of learning, the better the carryover to game night.

#52: Daily In-Season Practice Schedules

In an attempt to squeeze as much out of a week as possible, you will find through experience that you can "burnout" players the quickest, then assistant coaches, and finally you as head coach if you schedule too much for one practice week. Case in point: some coaches bring their team in on Saturday morning after a game on Friday night. They do some distance running, light weightlifting, and then watch the game video. This process could take two hours or more if they really get into critiquing the video. The players leave, but the coaching staff stays for another two hours to break down the game video and make plans for the week. Thus, on Saturday morning, they are at school for over four hours. Then they meet again on Sunday evening after trading videos with their next opponent and are in a meeting for two to three more hours. A better schedule would be to make Saturday a day of rest. Players and coaches both need time off to recharge their batteries. The coaches should have a staff meeting on Sunday evening and assistant coaches should be encouraged to have game DVDs at home to study, but you should pretty much take the weekend off.

Too many young head coaches tend to live by the old adage of "if a little is good, then *more* is better," which is another coaching myth that needs to be dispelled. There is a point of diminishing returns that a coach can encounter with his players and staff that can ruin a season and invariably ruin a program.

A detailed practice schedule should be prepared during the day of a particular practice and should be posted on the locker room bulletin board for all players to see before they head for the practice field (refer to Figure 5-1 for sample daily practice schedules). Every coach should have a copy of the schedule and refer to it numerous times during practice. Many coaches use the "five-minute period" type schedule. It is preferable to block out a 10-, 20-, 30- (or more) minute period, depending on the activity. Allow for 60 seconds to change periods and make sure that time is built into the schedule. If you have seven or eight different periods, you are adding seven minutes to your schedule, and if you don't account for them, you will run out of time. You should even include the time it takes to walk to the field from the locker room.

You should have a staff meeting after practice every day to review and plan for the next day. When coaches get home, if they are teachers, they have papers to grade and lesson plans to prepare, and they also need some time for their family. *No* correlation exists between the hours spent on football each week and the number of wins a school has each season. An organized coach can get more done in one hour than some coaches can accomplish in two or three.

	Monday	
Period	**Times**	**Activity**
Pre	3:55-4:09 p.m.	Bloopers
Pre	4:10 4:14 p.m.	Team meeting
Pre	4:15-4:24 p.m.	View current opponent's game video
Pre	4:25-4:34 p.m.	To field
1	4:35-4:44 p.m.	Team flex
2	4:45-4:50 p.m.	Punt and PAT/field goal
3	4:51 4:56 p.m.	Kickoff and field goal
4	4:57-5:17 p.m.	Offensive positions—fundamentals
5	5:18-5:39 p.m.	Defensive positions
6	5:40-6:04 p.m.	Team defense
	Managers: Turn on middle school lights!	
7	6:05-6:09 p.m.	To middle school field
8	6:10-6:34 p.m.	Team offense
9	6:35-6:44 p.m.	Go in to lift

Offensive Script

1	Fly 611 rocket
2	132
3	938
4	Strong jet 482 down
5	Strong jet 688 down
6	Strong hawk 481 quarterback follow
7	Strong hawk 689 quarterback follow
8	Zap 458 tar heel
9	Zap 653 pipe
10	484 dive
11	*484 dive pop pass*
12	Zap 683 keep pass
13	Zap 487 keep pass
14	Zap 481 down sweep keep
15	Zap 689 down sweep keep
16	Shot/Gun: 83/87 Nike wheel
17	Shot/Gun: 32/38 Nike
18	Shot/Gun: 32/38
19	Shot/Gun: 83/87
20	Shot/Gun: 83/87 Jersey mouse

Figure 5-1. Sample daily practice schedules

Tuesday

Period	Times	Activity
Pre	3:55-4:00 p.m.	Team meeting
Pre	4:01-4:14 p.m.	To field and specialties
1	4:15-4:24 p.m.	Team flex
2	4:25-4:31 p.m.	Punt block and PAT
3	4:32-4:38 p.m.	Kickoff return and field goal
4	4:39-5:04 p.m.	Buck sweep drill
5	5:05-5:14 p.m.	Offense groups—waggle/keep pass drill
6	5:15-5:34 p.m.	Offense groups—pass review: 90s; 60s; Nikes
7	5:35-5:54 p.m.	Defense
8	5:55-6:39 p.m.	Team offense
9	6:40-6:45 p.m.	Goal-line offense
		Staff meeting

Offensive Script

1	Heavy bench hawk 441 vs. 31 double walk-up
2	Heavy bench hawk 483 trk at 9 vs. 31 slant to motion
3	Strong 121/429 "check with me" vs. 31 linebacker's overshift
4	Jet 82/88 keep pass vs. 31 double walk-up
5	Fly 419 rocket vs. 31 double walk-up
6	Hawk 92/98
7	Fly 936/134 center pass

A	Strong 21/29—"check with me" vs. 31 linebacker's off set
B	Hawk 92/98

8	Roll-to 483 dbl. dive vs. 31 double walk-up Baker
9	832 vs. 31 wide end on tight end
10	F 82/88 keep pass vs. 31 double walk-up
11	Hawk 94/96 "under" vs. 31 double walk-up "B"
12	Fly 83/87 quarterback follow vs. 31 double walk-up "A"
13	122 bruin trap vs. 31 double walk-up
14	Hawk 93/97 vs. 31 double walk-up Baker

C	832 vs. 31 wide defensive end on tight end
D	928 Bruin trap vs. 31 double walk-up

15	Shot/Gun: 61/69 vs. 22 loose
16	Shot/Gun: 32/38 Nike vs. 22 loose
17	Shot/Gun: 83/87 vs. 22 loose
18	Shot/Gun: 83/87 jersey mouse vs. 22 loose "B"
19	Shot/Wing: 72/78 bench vs. 31 over
20	Shot/Wing: 83/87 follow vs. 31 over
21	Shot/Wing: 34/36 center pass vs. 31 over

Figure 5-1. Sample daily practice schedules (cont.)

Wednesday		
Period	**Times**	**Activity**
Pre	3:55-4:09 p.m.	Weightlifting
Pre	4:10-4:19 p.m.	View current opponent's game video (Coach Walker: watch clock)
Pre	4:20-4:29 p.m.	To field
1	4:30-4:35 p.m.	Punt and PAT
2	4:36-4:41 p.m.	Kickoff & field goal
3	4:42-4:55 p.m.	Pursuit drill
4	4:56-5:00 p.m.	Water
5	5:01-5:09 p.m.	Defensive groups
6	5:10-5:19 p.m.	Defensive groups—linebackers switch
7	5:20-5:44 p.m.	7-on-7 and pass rush/trap drill
8	5:45-6:09 p.m.	Team offense—pass
9	6:10-6:44 p.m.	Team offense
10	6:45-6:50 p.m.	Goal-line defense

Offensive Script

1	Fly 683 keep pass vs. 22 walk-up strong/x Abel/A
2	Fly 487 keep pass vs. 22 walk-up strong/x Abel/A
3	124 trap vs. 22 x Abel/A
4	121/929 waggle vs. 22 b
5	Fly 429/621 waggle vs. 22 Baker/B
6	Jet 482/688 down vs. 22 walk-up strong Baker/B
7	Jet 482/688 keep pass vs. 22 walk-up strong
—	
A	Fly 683 keep pass vs. 22 walk-up strong/x Abel/A
B	Jet 688 keep pass vs. 22 walk-up strong Baker
—	
8	Hawk 91/99 vs. 22 x Abel/A
9	Hawk 93/97 vs. 22 Baker/B
10	Hawk 91/99 hitch and roll vs. 22 Baker/B
11	Hawk 483/687 vs. 22 Baker/B
12	Shot/Wing: 91/99 split end screen vs. 22 Abel/A
13	Shot/Wing: 34/36 center vs. 22
14	Shot/Wing: 73/77 pipe
—	
C	Hawk 91/99 hitch and roll vs. 22 Abel/A
D	Hawk 93/97 vs. 22 x Abel/A
—	
15	Shot/Gun: 65 sundance vs. 22 Baker
16	Shot/Gun: 65 back porch vs. 52 middle x
17	Shot/Gun: 83/87 jersey mouse vs. 52 middle x
18	Shot/Gun: 32/38 Nike vs. whip
19	Shot/Gun: 32/38 vs. 22 Batman
20	Shot/Gun: 63/67 vs. 22 Baker
21	Shot/Gun: 83/87 Nike

Figure 5-1. Sample daily practice schedules (cont.)

#53: Report Card

Post a "report card" each Monday on the locker room bulletin board. This card should be a *summary* of how you evaluated the team's performance from the previous Friday night after watching the game video. Do not include individual grades on the report card. Giving individual grades for game performance is time-consuming and generally doesn't improve anyone's performance. Individual grading is only effective if you can afford to bench a starter when his game performance is consistently graded as below average or failing. It makes little sense to consistently give a starter a failing grade if the only guy behind him is, for example, a sophomore who is not ready to play in a varsity game. In this type of situation, an individual grading system will be looked at as a joke among the players. Spending time on the practice field trying to correct the mistakes you've viewed on the game video is much more valuable than spending hours grading each starter's individual performance on every play.

On the report card, comment about how each kicking team and the offensive and defensive positions played and then grade each of those groups on execution and effort. Conclude with an evaluation of the overall team performance—again, grading them on execution and effort. On the team summary, you should make general comments about why you won (or lost) based on your execution and hustle. In this manner, no one person will get blame or accolades. It's a team effort that is recognized.

The first thing your players will do on Monday when they come in the locker room is go straight to the bulletin board and check their grade. Read the report during your meeting time before practice and let the coaches add any comments they feel are appropriate. Then post the report card back on the bulletin board, where it remains all week.

The report card will also indicate whether a team (offense, defense, and/or kicking team) met their game objective for the week. The players on those teams will know on Monday if they are going to be rewarded with their helmet sticker during the ceremony on Thursday. Figure 5-2 provides a sample report card.

Report Card vs. Phoebus

Offensive line: We showed improvement in our ability to stay on blocks. We still need work on getting on (and staying on) linebackers when our job is to get to the second level. The pass blocking was good. Our angles on trap blocks and the effort of getting down field were very good.
Effort: B+   Execution: B-

Running backs: We ran hard and made good cuts most of the night. We still need work on our blocking from halfbacks and wingbacks on down blocks and reaches. Motion and alignment also need work.
Effort: A-   Execution: C+

Receivers: Our patterns still need to be sharper. We made the catches (except one) that we had to make. Our blocking improved but the split ends still need to improve on their stalk blocks.
Effort: B+   Execution: B-

Quarterbacks: A solid performance by both quarterbacks. We made good decisions for the most part and there were no critical errors. Pete should have stayed in the pocket a little longer, but overall, "ran the show" really well. Execution, faking, and play-calling were very good.
Effort: A-   Execution: B+

Offensive summary: We took advantage of the field position that the kicking teams gave us and we only had one stalled drive in the "green zone." We ran the ball well against a strong defensive unit. We need to continue to "sharpen up" our timing—particularly our "gamecock" package. We will expand the offense when the coaches feel you have a complete understanding of what we have installed so far.
Effort: B+   Execution: B-

Defensive line: We got knocked around way too much on their first drive. But once they got into the goal-line situation, we rose up and shut them down—great goal-line stand! Once we got the speed of the game, we played much more solidly. We need to stay lower coming up the field. We ran the circle really well—especially Quintrell!
Effort: B   Execution: B-

Linebackers: We stepped up inside a few times and got cut off from running downhill to the off-tackle or sweep plays. But the effort was good and we were around the ball all night. The pass coverage must improve.
Effort: B   Execution: B-

Figure 5-2. Sample report card

Secondary: We didn't get tested too much on the deep ball, but it was good practice for coming up in run support. We had very few coverage breakdowns and we ran to the ball well. We will see an entirely different attack next week.
Effort: B+   Execution: B+

Defensive summary: Once we got warmed up, we controlled them for the most part. They played their back-up quarterback, but it was our ability to stop the run that was most impressive, as that's their forte. We are definitely on schedule to becoming a dominating defensive unit. The errors we made that allowed long runs were once again two people in the same gap Linemen: use your speed and strength to defeat opponents. If you stand up, you will get whipped. We're just a couple of mistakes away from being really good!
Effort: B   Execution: B-

Special teams: Once again, our emphasis on special teams paid off in a big way: touchdown on the kickoff return; punt block set up two scores; field goal block forced a bad kick that kept them from scoring on the first drive; punt coverage didn't allow #38 to get open; kickoffs were good and coverage was strong; and we hit all of our PATs! It was a dominating performance!
Effort: A-   Execution: A-

Overall team performance: We answered a lot of questions with last Thursday's performance. The veterans led by example and the rookies showed that we can compete with anyone—when we execute. We went "toe-to-toe" with them physically. We will be the "little guys" all season, but remember, "It's not the size of the dog in the fight; it's the size of the fight in the dog that counts!" Nice work!
Effort: B+   Execution: B-

Note: the coaches consider it a "winning performance" only if you score a grade of B or higher. Don't be satisfied with anything less!

Figure 5-2. Sample report card (cont.)

#54: Bloopers Video

Instead of showing the entire game on Monday before practice (and using a lot of time that you could devote to practice), make a "bloopers" video that shows the major errors that players committed during the game—a "cut-up" video of "lowlights"—a video of all the mistakes that your team made during the game. Set the timer for 20 minutes and when it goes off, you are done. This timeframe forces the coaches to make quick and concise comments about the blooper being shown. Show the lowlight once and move on. Then get out on the field and correct the mistakes.

The mistakes that you see on the video are the things that your position coaches will correct when they go to the individual period on Monday practices. Don't waste valuable time reviewing game tape with your players, criticizing and berating them, when that time spent in the film room could be devoted to on-the-field correction time.

#55: Scouting Reports

Distributing a scouting report to your players on Monday is a critical element in game preparation. This report is as important to the coordinator as it is for the players. To know your opponent is to be prepared to take advantage of his weaknesses. Many games can be "won" on Monday—long before your team takes the field on Friday night. The first page of the scouting report should include a summary of what you expect the opponent to do and a list of comments (see Figure 5-3). The scouting report should also include a list of the jersey numbers and alignment of the opponent's players. A page of defensive fronts you expect to see is another key piece of your offense's scouting report.

For your defensive scouting report, diagram the opponent's five favorite running plays and their three favorite pass plays. When you review the report before practice on Monday, emphasize to the players that these are the plays that you must stop if you want to be successful on defense. Then, show a few minutes of your opponent's game video just so your players can get a preliminary look at who they will be competing against. If your next opponent is much weaker than your team, make a highlight tape of positive plays that your opponent has made. Point out to your team when you watch it that, "These guys can make plays if you let them." It's an effective way of keeping your team from getting overconfident. If your next opponent is stronger than you, make a cut-up tape of their bloopers. Show your kids that these guys are human and they make mistakes. If you capitalize on those mistakes, you can frustrate them and you have a chance to upset them.

Scouting Report vs. Oscar Smith
(Regional Playoffs)

- They will run an odd front defense against us with their inside linebackers tight to the line. They will walk up the strong safety to our tight end/wing back flank and play him on the line.
- The inside linebackers will blitz some. We must be ready to cut off their penetration. The offside linebacker on the line will not blitz.
- The secondary will play mostly three deep and keep everything in front of them. They will walk the free safety up and play some man.
- When we go to shotgun, they will blitz. It's more of a 2-deep secondary—and the defensive line will shade toward our flex end strength side.
- They will blitz when it gets to be third down and long.
- They want to take away our tight end/wingback flank running game. They are committing extra defenders to that side.

Comments:

- We are a much better offense than the one they played in September. We block better up front and are executing our game plans much more effectively.
- They feel like they beat us once and they can do so again with little trouble. Their big game is next week against Salem—we're just "roadkill" on the way to Virginia Beach.
- We will mix in a few "tricks" and throw the ball on first down more often. We need to give Kevin time to find a receiver and follow through.

Figure 5-3. Sample scouting report summary

#56: Lieutenants' Weekly Meetings

Plan to meet with your team leaders every Monday night after practice. Start with a brief review of a leadership trait that you want to emphasize to your cadre and then talk about the team. The question you always want to pose to the lieutenants as they arrive in the meeting room is, "Is there anything going on that I need to know about?" If there is an issue that you should deal with, you have to be able to count on your lieutenants to bring it to your attention. That's why it's important to explain to them at the pre-season lunch meeting when they accepted the title that they must be your "eyes and ears" in the locker room, around the school, and in the community. They are the "go-betweens" between the players and you. If they cannot perform this duty, they will not be allowed to continue as a team leader.

If there is a particular concern brought to your attention by a lieutenant, you need to hash it out right there before you leave. For example, during homecoming week, you want to always emphasize to the lieutenants to tell the team that their job is to play the game on Friday night—not to help with the homecoming preparations. Often players will listen to their peers and they cast a deaf ear on what the coaches are saying to them. Utilize your leadership team as that conduit between the staff and the team.

#57: Bullhorn to Change Practice Periods

A student manager should be assigned to do nothing else during your practices but to keep tabs of the practice schedule and time periods. When a period ends, it is the manager's job to blow the horn and announce when a new period starts, which will keep practice on schedule and running smoothly. Every coach should keep a copy of the practice schedule with him. When a horn blows, he must check his schedule to be sure he is coaching the right drill during the right period.

You will probably need to train your student managers on how to read the schedule, as most of them don't understand the difference between individual period and conditioning. Work with them until you find two students who grasp what the schedule means and assign them the duty of keeping time and blowing the bullhorn. You don't want confusion as to when the horn should blow or, again, you will get off schedule. Have extra batteries stored in your office in case the horn dies during practice.

#58: Conditioning in the Middle of Practice

Some coaches are disturbed by the lack of real effort being put forth by their players during practice. It sometimes appears as if they are holding back or "saving" something. If you sit down with some veterans in the off-season and ask them about this situation, you will find that the majority of them will say the same thing: "Coach, we always knew we had a lot of running to do at the end of practice. We didn't want to push it too hard during practice, so we'd have something left for conditioning at the end."

If this effort is an issue with your team, then you need to move conditioning toward the beginning of practice. The players are fresher, and, once conditioning is done, they can focus on the practice itself. Therefore, on the daily practice schedule conditioning should come right after team flex and kicking game. You will get a good 10- to 12-minute conditioning period and then take a four-minute break, where they can get to the sideline, get off their feet, get some water, and get their heart rate back down. Once you blow the horn to head back on the field, everyone should be ready to focus on the rest of practice. The players will soon come to realize that with no conditioning at the end of practice, they do not need to "hold back" any longer. It will make your practices a lot crisper and you will see a lot more effort put forth by everyone.

#59: Water on the Practice Field

Purchase 18 to 24 16 oz. squirt bottles. Make it the responsibility of the student managers and trainers to fill the bottles with water and move around the field throughout practice with the bottles in their carrying cases. If a player is not actively involved in a drill, he is allowed to get a drink of water from one of the bottles and then immediately return to practice. This system reduces or even eliminates the need to take several time-consuming water breaks and allows the players to get as much water as they want throughout practice.

You should also require each player to bring his own big jug of ice water to practice each day. If you have a prolonged break where the players come off the field, they can drink from their own water container. Be cautious about allowing them to share containers as it can lead to germs being spread among the players.

#60: Pre-Game Practice Script

Like a director preparing his actors for the opening night of a play, you want your players to "rehearse" all the possible situations that could arise in a game. You should "play a game" on Thursday practice. The schedule should be set up to follow the ebb and flow of a typical game. Script all the possible things that could occur so you have properly prepared for anything that might happen during a game (Figure 5-4).

Start with the opening kickoff return. It is just a "run through," not live, but make sure that you have the correct 11 on the field and that they know how to form up your return. Blow the whistle when the back gets around the 35 and then bring the offense out on the field with a scout defense carrying shields. Run three or four plays that have been scripted and let the back go the distance on the last play so that he scores. Then bring the PAT team on to kick the extra point. From there, the kickoff team comes on and rehearses your kickoff and coverage. The offensive scout team comes out and runs three plays against your starting defense, and then the punt block team comes out and the scout team punts to them.

You can be as creative as you want to keep the kids "in the zone." You may yell out on second down that someone has hurt his leg and you need his backup on the field. That player should make a big production of limping off the field while you wait to see if his backup was paying attention and gets on the field in a timely fashion. Be sure to rehearse what you do on a safety, whether kicking or receiving. Also rehearse what happens during overtime. Take a break, call the team up like you would on game night when regulation is over, and explain what happens now that you are going into overtime. You should even practice the overtime coin toss so there are no questions. This is a great time to work on your two minute offense versus "air." Let your offense move down the field against a running clock to set up for the game-winning field goal.

You don't want any surprises on game night. Remember, this practice is not live contact, although you should wear shoulder pads to provide some protection. You should cover any and all phases of the game so the players are mentally prepared for anything that might come up during the game. As the head coach, you should be confident that you have exposed your team to all variables that they may face on Friday night.

Pre-Game Practice Script

1	Kickoff return	13	Kickoff
2	Offense	14	Defense (three plays)
	•	15	Field goal/kick block
	•	16	Kickoff return
	•	17	Backed-up offense
	•		•
3	PAT		•
4	Kickoff		•
5	Defense (four plays)	18	Tight punt
6	Punt block	19	Goal-line defense (four plays)
7	Offense	20	Goal-line offense (gamecock)
	•		•
	•		•
	•		•
	•		•
8	Punt	21	Safety kick/punt
9	Defense (four plays)	22	Safety return
10	Punt return	23	Scramble drill (hail Mary plays)
11	Offense	24	Onside kickoff return
	•	25	Two-minute drill
	•	26	Two-point play
	•	27	Overtime!
12	Field goal		

Figure 5-4. Pre-game practice script

#61: Video Breakdown

Up-to-date video equipment is necessary for analyzing your team and your opponents. Be sure to emphasize the importance of obtaining this equipment to your athletic director and principal.

As discussed elsewhere in this chapter, video of your own team should be reviewed to evaluate team performance (#53: Report Card) and to identify both "lowlights" (#54: Bloopers Video) and highlights (#63: Highlight Video). At the high school level, it's also important for an offensive coordinator to spend time evaluating his play calling. He must look to be sure that he is not becoming too predictable in calling (e.g., play-action passes on first down).

When looking at an opponent's game video, one of the key things to evaluate is tendencies; every team and every coach has them. Identifying your opponent's tendencies can be of tremendous help in developing your game plan and showing your players that you have something they can take advantage of. For example, when a linebacker is going to blitz, does he step up and tap the defensive lineman in front of him on a particular hip? This action not only indicates that he is going to blitz, but also tells you which gap he is going to come through.

It is also important to evaluate each player on the opposing team. You want to find out who the "weakest link" is on their defense. You can exploit the weak link at a key point in the game. This portion of your video breakdown will require a lot of time but it is worth it.

Make sure you spend enough time evaluating your opponent to develop an effective scouting report and game plan that will be presented to your staff and players for your upcoming game. Today, the preferred mode of scouting is by video. You can review a play as many times as necessary to get the information that you need when watching a game video. If possible, you should also try to send a coach to scout teams at live games, because valuable information can be gathered in person that you can't get from watching film.

#62: Ceremony

The ceremony is held after the pre-game practice day (usually Thursday). Get the team seated in the locker room or your meeting room and start by showing the highlight video from your previous game. During the video, everyone is required to applaud and cheer for the player who is being highlighted on any given play. If they don't clap loud enough (or enthusiastically enough), stop the projector and have a little talk about how this procedure is a "unity" and "respect" thing and you expect everyone to get involved. The applause will create an air of camaraderie that will build your team into a true "band of brothers." There will be a lot of laughter and enthusiasm as they enjoy seeing the big plays that everyone made in the game.

The next phase of the ceremony is the awarding of helmet stickers. Start with the team awards (offense, defense, and individual kicking teams). If a particular team achieved their game objective then that team is called forward and everyone applauds as they walk up. The coordinator for that team will say a few words about how they achieved their objectives and then he awards the stickers to each individual player. As that team returns to their seats, the rest of the team should applaud.

Next, individual "big play" stickers are awarded. If a player earns multiple stickers, you should announce why he earned each one. Write down the player's name and what he did as you are recording the highlight video on Sunday. Then you have a list to follow and recite when it's time to present the stickers on Thursday. It is gratifying when a backup, who only got in for the last series, can be called up and cheered on by his teammates for making a big play during his brief time on the field.

To conclude the ceremony, you will give your pre-game pep talk. Your talk should revolve around your "word of the week," which you've emphasized the last four days. Your "word of the week" is selected on Sunday so you can post it in the locker room before practice on Monday.

It is preferable to get your players charged up on Thursday evening, rather than before the game on Friday. Emotions will be high before a game anyway. Raising their emotional level on Thursday before they go home allows them to think about what you said throughout the evening and in school the next day. When talking to them before you take the field on Friday night, emphasize being focused and intense, yet not being out of control emotionally when they play. It will help to keep your players on an even keel during the game. Teams that are sky high to start a game will hit an emotional wall around halftime. It is difficult to raise that emotional level again for the start of the second half. At this time, point out to your team that because they came out focused and under control, they can take the battle to their opponent in the second half and wear them out.

#63: Team Objectives

Team objectives are the goals that your coaches set down for each special team (and offense and defense) that the particular team must achieve in the game in order to earn their helmet sticker (Figure 5-5). Develop these objectives based on the concept of what your coaches feel it would take execution-wise to be successful. If the offense, for instance, achieves their game objective, it means that the offense played well and your chances of winning the game are vastly improved. You should have objectives for offense, defense, and all of your kicking teams. Get your charts laminated and posted on the locker room wall, then when you have your ceremony on Thursdays, review the chart and the objectives with the team to see if any particular teams achieve their minimum goal.

Sample Team Objectives

Offensive Team Game Objectives
(The team must earn +7 points or more to earn their sticker.)

Objective		Points Earned
Drive batting average	.333	+3
Drive batting average	.667	+1 (bonus)
Total yards	300	+1
Third down conversion	50% or higher	+2
Three and out series	2 or less	+1
Turnovers	1 or less	+2
Big plays (15 yards—run 25 yards—pass)	4 or more	+1
Violent yards	4.0 yards/carry	+1
Pass completion	50%	+1
Penalties	25 yards or less	+1
Foolish penalties		-1

Defensive Team Game Objectives
(The team must earn +7 points or more to earn their sticker.)

Objective		Points Earned
Drive batting average	.150 or less	+3
Shut-out	.000	+1 (bonus)
Total yards	Less than 150	+1
Three and out series	5	+2
Third down conversion	50%	+1
Turnovers	3	+2
Leads to score		+1 (bonus)
Big plays (> 25 yards)	2 or less	+1
Pass completion	40%	+1
Penalties	25 yards or less	+1
Foolish penalties		-1

Kickoff Team Game Objectives

- Ideally, no returns past the 30
- Less than five-yard return if the ball is fielded past the 30
- No missed tackles
- No penalties
- All 11 players hustling in their lanes
- Bonus award: stop inside 15-yard line or turnover
- Double bonus: touchdown

Figure 5-5. Sample team objectives

#64: Highlight Video

As previously mentioned, it is important to show your highlight video to your team during the ceremony after your Thursday practice. A key point is: regardless of whether you won or lost the previous game, you *must* still show the highlight video to your team. There are always big plays and great effort that you want to emphasize to your team. This video can be a great learning tool after a loss because your players are smart enough to see that with a few more big plays at the right time, they probably could have won that particular game. It also emphasizes that your purpose for playing football is more than just winning games. Players will be emotionally strengthened when they see that even though they lost, their coach wants to highlight big plays that were made. By showing it on Thursday, the last thing the team sees before game day is their success from the week before—regardless of whether they won or lost that previous game. The positive images have a strong effect on the mind-set of your young players.

Cut up the video on Sunday right after completing the blooper tape, which means watching the game tape twice, but is also a great way to self scout.

#65: Game Plan and Ready List

The final stage of proper preparation is having your game plan down on paper and constructing your ready list, or playsheet, for the game (Figures 5-6 and 5-7). The focus, in this instance, is on offense. Knowledge of how to attack defenses with your offense and a plan of exploiting your opponent's weaknesses are crucial to putting the ball in the end zone. A ready list must include plays that you have pre-determined to call when you get in "crunch time" situations (i.e., third and short, backed-up offense inside your own five-yard line, or a two-point play you might need to call to win the game). You don't want to have to be thinking about these things as the game unfolds.

Some coaches are advocates of "scripting" the first 10 or 20 plays. Scripting can help in learning important information about your opponent as the game opens, but it limits you in terms of plays you might want to call.

Based on scouting your opponent and seeing what has been most effective during practice during the week, you should create a ready list of key plays that you want to emphasize throughout the game. An alternative form of scripting would be to use several different formations during your first series on offense, which will give your staff an idea of how the other teams will align against you. You have to run your "Big 5" plays to see what is working before you can settle into a rhythm in your play calling.

Complete your ready list the morning of your game. After writing up the game plan after practice on Thursday, take some time to decide which five plays you feel are best suited for attacking the defense you expect your opponent to use. You will have a good idea by then as to what you want to put on paper. Designate those key plays as your Big 5 plays for that game.

Game Plan vs. Deep Creek

- Our opponent will run primarily our 22 defense. They will change up to an odd front—especially if we go to shotgun. They will walk the outside linebacker up to our wingback flank. The inside linebackers will blitz occasionally, so you must keep your head up when you are blocking and protect your gap.
- They will play a three-deep zone secondary and give our split end plenty of room. We must hit them in the short to medium range and then burn them deep.
- Our attack will begin with what we do best: run buck sweep and get Kevin on the corners. We will flip to shift to run some at #80, but I have seen other teams run at #55 on 121 and he does not hold up to the constant pounding. Tight end: be ready for him to stunt inside you when he gets tired of getting beat on by our wingbacks.
- They do not align properly to our 200/800 formation—we must take advantage of this. We have 11/19 toss to the wing to attack the flank to the tight end side. The keep pass to that flank should be open also.
- Waggle will be effective. They will drop their outside linebackers to the flat, so Kevin has to be ready to cut it up—run down the "tunnel" and get downfield with the keep.
- We'll continue to hit them inside, then outside, and throw. We will go to shotgun and shot/wing early to see how they adjust. Once we find what they cannot stop, we will stay with it and crush them with it.
- When we go gamecock, backs should be ready to bounce the 31/39. Tight ends must stay on their blocks.

Keys to Victory

- *Eliminate turnovers.* We must not kill drives or give our defense bad field position by giving away the ball.
- *Score in the red zone.* They are a good defense and will fight hard to keep us out of the end zone. When we get close, we have to come away with at least three points. Remember: the 22-yard line is the magic number.
- *Protect the quarterback.* He needs time to complete passes. Stay on your man and pick up their blitzing linebackers.

Figure 5-6. Sample game plan

Ready List vs. Deep Creek

Big 5:
- Flip to 929/121
  - ✓ Roll to fly 429/621
  - ✓ Strong fly 621/429
- Fly 911/119 toss
  - ✓ Fly 219/811 toss
- Roll to strong 131/939 power
- Heavy bench trips 452/658 tar heel
- Hawk 691/499 hitch and roll
  - ✓ Hawk 694/496
- Backed-up offense:
- Roll to 483
- Flip to 929
- 496
- Silent sneak

Next 5:
- Tank fly 429 naked pass
  - ✓ Tank fly 429 naked run
  - ✓ Tank fly 429 hornet
- 132/938 down power
- 121/929 waggle and run
  - ✓ Fly 429/621 waggle and run
- (Short) fly 634 wingback counter
- 883/287 and KP

Auxiliary:
- 137/933 x-x
- 134/936 center
- Fly 134/936 center pass
- Roll-to fly 681/489 down sweep
- #12 heavy bench hawk 441 and pass and pop
- #12 heavy bench hawk 441 truck run to 9

Shotgun attack:
- 83/87 snowman
- 83/87
- Hokie 83/87 jersey mouse
- Hawk 91/99 "tiger"
- 64/66 go!
- 32/38 Nike

- 62/68
- 24/26 trap
- Spread 93/97
- 63/67 and "fin"

Shot wing attack:
- 31/39 sweep pass
- 83/87 follow
- 24/26 trap
- 22/28
- 34/36 center
- 72/78 bench

Third and short (1-3):
- Roll to 483
- Zap 683/487
- 883 KP

Third and medium (4-8):
- Heavy bench trips
- 929 waggle and run
- Tank fly 429 hornet/pass
- S/W: 31/39 sweep pass

Third and long (9+):
- S/G: 32/38 Nike
- S/G: 64/66 go!
- S/G: hawk 91/99 tiger
- S/G: 65 sundance

Goal line:
- 24/26 on
- 32/38
- 31/39
- 83 ranger
- 83/87

Two-point play:
- Roll to strong 929
- Roll to 929 waggle. Run (split end crack block)
- S/G: 83/87 jersey mouse

Figure 5-7. Sample ready list (playsheet)

#66: Emphasis on Kicking Game

Many games are won because of the success of the kicking game. Send this message to your players by starting your practice each day with a particular phase of the kicking game. Starting practice with the kicking game emphasizes that it is a crucial part of your success. Do not relegate it to some period in the middle of practice where you quickly run through it and move on.

Work on your kickoff and punt twice a week (Monday and Wednesday) because the execution of these two kicking teams is a little more involved. A mistake on either of these teams can result in a major momentum shift in the game. The kickoff return and punt block should be practiced on Tuesdays in detail and then reviewed on Thursdays. However, PAT and field goal must be practiced *every* day. While the other special teams are practicing at one end of the field, your PAT personnel should be down at the end zone kicking every day for 15 minutes. The timing and blocking is crucial for place kicks and you want as many reps as you can get every day. It will not always be live blocking, but you want that snap, hold, and kick to be practiced over and over.

#67: Quirks of Your Kicking Game

As vital as the kicking game will be to your success, you should consider an unconventional kicking-game style of play. For instance, an unconventional kickoff can drive opponents crazy and be a great opportunity for you to "steal" a turnover. You can kickoff from one hash and pop up the ball to the opposite outside third of the field (i.e., "skying" the ball from one hash mark and dropping it down on the numbers outside the opposite hash marks, which will create a number of chances to recover the kick without having to resort to an onside kick). Your kicker aims for the opposite 30-yard line. If you get enough hang time (and the longer the better), there is almost always no return. If there is, the returner will get plastered by your coverage players. If your opponent overcompensates and places too many personnel outside the hash, your kicker should turn around and kick a low line drive right down the middle of the field. That oblong ball will take some crazy bounces.

Photo credit: Doug Benc/Getty Images

Your punt block team should be just that—a *block* team. Do not waste time working on intricate returns. Most high school punters don't kick well enough to warrant using precious practice time to set up a return. Put 10 men on the line in sprinters' stances and go after the punter in an attempt to get the punt or get *to* the punter. You want to rattle this high school kicker into shanking the kick or popping the ball straight up. You will get the net yardage you want off of bad kicks or blocks.

Put 10 men on the line in sprinters' stances and bring them hard every time. You can learn a lot about the technique of blocking punts by talking with coach Frank Beamer at Virginia Tech. He has some excellent ideas on how to block punts. Bring the heat and watch your opponents wilt.

Have one kickoff return that you constantly repeat in practice. You don't have a lot of time to work on kickoff returns so become proficient at one thing. Set a goal to return at least one kickoff for a touchdown each season.

Always have a "good hands" team ready. If you know that teams are not going to kick it deep to you, you're better prepared to return a kick with 11 skilled players on the field. When you need them for a key onside kick attempt by your opponent late in a game, those kids have already been on the field.

You can win many games over the years if you are better prepared and execute your kicking teams more effectively than your opponent. The kicking game is the third of the game that a lot of coaches pay lip service to (as far as how important it is to them), however, they do not devote the time to making it a truly equal one-third of the game. It is in the kicking game that a coach who has a less-talented team can "steal" a win. Proper preparation in the kicking game means really paying attention to details. Did you know, for instance, that you can attempt a field goal after fair-catching a punt? And the defense cannot rush your kicker. Know the rule book concerning the kicking game. A lot of nuances in the kicking game will help you level the playing field. Keep in mind that in a close game between two evenly-matched teams, more than likely a mistake in the kicking game will determine the outcome.

#68: In-Season Weight Lifting

Don't learn the hard way that you need to continue to lift during the season. Lifting during the season is the key to sustaining the strength that the players will build up during your off-season program. It is imperative that your players lift at least twice a week during the season. As the season wears on, in-season weight lifting actually becomes a big part of the conditioning for your players. Don't forsake the weight room during the season. Make time for it—it will pay dividends.

If it's available at your school, encourage your players to register for the advanced PE class in weight training so they can get their lifting done during the day. Anyone in advanced PE can dress and go home after practice. Require those players not in the class to stay and lift after practice on Monday and Wednesday. It will only take one year of seeing teammates leave early to get most of your players to sign up for the weight lifting PE class.

#69: In-Season Staff Meetings

Be very careful that you don't become a big fan of long staff meetings. Nothing affects staff morale more than too many meetings. Be sure that you have an agenda and stick to it. It seems that a lot of time is wasted shooting the breeze when you could be finished and your staff can go home. It is recommended that you take it upon yourself to be sure that your meetings start on time and last no more than two hours. If the meeting lasts longer, you're not going to accomplish much more.

Proper preparation *before* the meeting is crucial. The coaches must come prepared by looking at their positions and evaluating their players from the previous game. Everyone should take a preliminary view of the upcoming opponent before the whole staff sits down together. As head coach, you can do game video breakdowns on Saturdays, however, you should give your assistant coaches the day off, then all of your staff should meet on Sunday evenings.

Start with a review of the previous game. The staff should watch the entire blooper tape you have put together and then discuss personnel. At this time, you can also discuss possible personnel changes. Talk about what you need to correct and what the point of emphasis will be during the coming week in practice and meetings.

You should also watch the highlight tape. Upon completion, read out to your staff those players who made "big plays" and thus will be awarded helmet stickers at the ceremony on Thursday, which will promote discussion of how to best utilize those players who are performing well for you.

Once your evaluation of your previous game is completed and you have discussed personnel, the next phase of the meeting is to begin to prepare for your upcoming opponent. Watch some game tape of your opponent and jot down notes. Have a scouting report already prepared on this team so that you can begin to get into some detail as to how you best feel you can defeat them. Ask your defensive coordinator this question: "What, in your estimation, are the three running plays and two passing plays that we need to stop to beat these guys?" His response is where the focus of defensive practice should be for the next week. After the staff leaves, continue to break down video and write up the scouting report. As head coach, you have to oversee all aspects of your program.

Remember, it is important to come into the meeting with an agenda that states the times that different subjects will be covered. You may need to be a "sergeant at arms" for awhile to be sure that your staff stays on task. As head coach, make sure that you ask for input from your assistants. Always tell them, "I am available to listen. I may not always agree with what you have to say, but I want to hear your ideas."

Other staff meetings concerns are "complainers" and negative attitudes. It must be a stated policy that if an assistant coach does not like the way something is being done, he can't bring up his complaint unless he brings a plan of action on how to solve the problem. As head coach, make sure to stay focused and positive.

#70: Copies of Opponents' Game Videos

Be sure to have one assistant coach who is highly skilled with video equipment. Make it his responsibility to make copies of the video to distribute to coaches and players. You will find that a player can get a lot more out of watching an opponent at home after he's finished his homework than taking time away from the practice field to watch the video. Suggest that players who live close to each other meet before school to watch it and make sure that your offensive and defensive starters get to see it during the week. Watching the video should be mandatory; include a written quiz in the scouting report to reinforce the necessity of reviewing the scouting video. Make it the players' responsibility to bring their DVDs back to the scouting coordinator on Thursday or they will not receive a new one on the following Monday.

6

Games

Preparing your team for a game is similar to actors preparing for that one big performance on stage when the curtain opens. This chapter discusses some things that will help any football coach prepare his team for their "night on Broadway." All of the preparation comes down to two hours of performing on the big stage where execution and effort will carry the day. Many *little things* that a successful coach must do on game night will spell victory or defeat. The better prepared you are to take care of the details, the better your chances are for success.

#71: Game Day Ritual

It is important to have a routine on game day that does not vary unless absolutely necessary. High school players are like thoroughbred race horses in that they are jittery before their performance and need the continuity of familiarity to help them stay focused. Providing a schedule from the time the final bell rings to end the school day until the whistle blows to kick off the game is important to maintain a high level of concentration and enthusiasm. To create the pre-game schedule, start with the kickoff time and backtrack to the start of your pre-game routine, filling in the appropriate times based on how many minutes are needed for each pre-game activity, as shown in Figure 6-1.

A number of things need to be part of the game day ritual. Each coach must decide what's important to him and then see that it's carried out every week. Kids need to know what to expect so that they can maintain their emotional state during the four to five hours before kickoff. Knowing what to expect is a critical element in how the team will perform during the game.

Pre-Game Schedule	
7:00 p.m.	Kickoff
6:55 p.m.	Team on sideline
6:50 p.m.	Line up under goal posts—take the field
6:40 p.m.	Finish pre-game warm-ups—leave field
6:33 p.m.	Team offense
6:26 p.m.	Team defense
6:23 p.m.	Punt and PAT teams
6:19 p.m.	Defensive positions
6:15 p.m.	Offensive positions
6:07 p.m.	Team flex
5:57 p.m.	Passing game
5:50 p.m.	Kicking specialists
5:40 p.m.	Special teams check—on bench
5:05 p.m.	Meetings and dress/video
4:55 p.m.	Walk the field
4:30 p.m.	Nap time
4:10 p.m.	Report to stadium

Figure 6-1. Sample pre-game schedule

#72: Pre-Game Meal

You can get a pre-game meal for your players in a number of ways. Whatever you do, one thing remains constant—athletes, especially teenagers, need a meal three to four hours before game time. How you accomplish getting them fed is up to you, but make sure they eat. The more nutritional value the meal has, the better for the athlete, however, it's better to have something in a player's stomach than to have nothing at all.

One option for pre-game meals is to take the team to a local restaurant. Another option is to bring Subway® sandwiches to the school and eat in the cafeteria as a team. You can also have the booster club serve a pre-game meal at the school.

Consider asking your school's nutrition class to prepare pre-game bag-lunch-type meals for players who want to participate. Work with the nutrition teacher on making it a fundraiser for her department, by having the players pay a small fee for the meals. Or, see if you can find a local businessman who is willing to subsidize the cost for the season (in exchange for free advertising in the game programs or a PA announcement during the games), resulting in free meals for the team and money for the nutrition department. The players should pick up their meals after school and proceed to the locker room, where they can eat together. This ritual promotes team unity by bringing the players together in a familiar place week after week. It also omits the worry of timing before the game, as the players will already be in the locker room.

#73: Nap Time

After evaluating his record over a five-year period, one coach was surprised to discover that his team actually had a higher winning percentage on the road than they did at home. This statistic was perplexing to him, since most teams hope to have that "home-field advantage" and win most of their games in front of their own fans. He began to explore factors that distinguished what they did on the road that were different from what they did at home. The one factor that stood out was: on road games they took the bus. On bus rides, the players had to remain absolutely silent once they pulled out of the school parking lot. Many of the players used this time on the ride to away games to sleep. Others sat quietly and listened to music but everyone was still and quiet for 20 to 30 minutes, which was not the case at home games. At home, they would have meetings and a lot of sit-around time that basically allowed the players to lose their edge. The solution: a quiet time before home games.

After they are finished eating, the team should clean up the trash from the meal and then all starters are required to stay in the locker room. Backups are allowed to stay if they choose to, but anyone who stays in the locker room is required to be absolutely still and quiet for 25 minutes for "nap time." Reserves who don't want to stay for nap time will go to the weight room or sit outside in the stands, but starters have to take a nap. The players should grab a blocking shield for a pillow, get settled on the floor, or set up some sort of bed using chairs and blocking dummies, and then you turn off the lights. During this time, the coaches meet in the coach's office adjacent to the locker room to do a last-minute review of the game plan and to relax a few minutes. "Nap time" will have a tremendous effect on your players' mental acuity in preparation for your home games.

#74: Walk the Field

One tradition during your pre-game ritual that you should establish is to walk the game field prior to every game. If you are the visitor, the first thing you should do after getting off the buses is to meet with your team under the nearest goal post. As your team gathers in the end zone, talk to them about "staking your territory" and not giving up one inch, even though you are on foreign soil. The entire team and staff then walk down the length of the field. Caution your players that if your opponent has gone to a lot of trouble to paint their field and make it look nice, not to disrespect their hosts by defacing the field. Their field and how it looks is obviously a focus of pride for that school. Disrespecting the opponent's hard work is a way to get them even more determined to play hard and win. Don't give your opponent any edge that you can control from your standpoint.

For home games, the walk is a little different. After waking the starters from their nap, your players and coaches head out to the track at the end of the home stands and meet up with any team members who did not lie down. Lead the way across the track and walk up the back of the end zone, proceed through the goal posts, and down the field. Stop at the 50-yard line and gather around your team emblem painted in the middle of your stadium field. No one is allowed to step on the emblem. Everyone is required to walk around it until the entire team has encircled it.

Share a few motivational remarks about "being here before." Kids all like the line from the commercial that "this is *our* house." Remind them of the significance of this particular game and talk about what the emblem you're gathered around represents and the pride it holds for all past teams. It is just a one- to two-minute time of inspiration. Next comes one of the most effective motivational activities that you will ever do—it is the key point in time in your pre-game ritual: tell each of your players and coaches to reach down and "grab some gold" (or silver or whatever color your school emblem is painted). Each team member will grab a few blades of painted grass and continue their march down to the far end zone and sprinkle the "gold" in that end zone.

Once you complete your walk of the game field, head for your team area (at away games) or back to the locker room (at home). Then, finish dressing and proceed to commence with your pre-game warm-ups.

#75: Special Teams Check-Up

When your players are finished dressing and the coaches have met with their players, walk out to your bench area for your special teams check. Skilled players should bring their helmet and shoulder pads with them, because they will not have time to go back to the locker room after the conclusion of the special teams check to get their pads.

Call out a particular kicking team. The coach who coordinates it lines them up, counts his men, calls for any backups, and gives a 30-second reminder to his players as to why their role in the game is important. After checking all special teams, then you call out the offense. Your offensive coordinator reminds them once again of the "keys to victory" as stated in the game plan (refer to #65: Game Plan and Ready List) and exhorts them to play hard and play smart. The defensive coordinator then does the same for his defensive starters. As they are finishing up, call for the kickers, snappers, and return men to take the field to begin pre-game kicking warm-ups. The rest of the team then heads back to the locker room or team area to finish last minute details and get ready to take the field for their portion of pre-game warm-ups.

This special team check-up will get your team out of the locker room and onto the field approximately 75 minutes before kickoff. Most people get tired of waiting for the game to start, so by getting everyone out on the sideline, the spectators begin to sense that the kickoff is drawing near. Once you start the special teams check, the countdown clock will be ticking. It is important that you use the backtrack method (refer to #71: Game Day Ritual) to be sure that you have set aside enough time to do everything you want to do as far as warming up before you leave the field to begin the game.

#76: Pre-Game Warm-Ups

The first players out on the field are the kicking specialists. You should give the kickers, snappers, and returners seven minutes to get off as many kicks as possible. Oftentimes, your place kicker will not be doing anything but kicking. He and the holder (or the kicker can use a tee) can continue to get off some field goals as the rest of the team runs through position drills. At seven minutes, any backs and receivers who are not already on the field as return men will begin to warm up and flex. They will then proceed to your 40-yard line and use the next 10 minutes to run patterns and let the quarterbacks warm up their arms. While they are throwing the ball, the remaining linemen meet in the end zone and begin to jog and stretch. When the next whistle blows, the whole team will rally in your end zone and begin to whoop it up. They then break out onto the field and line up for some quick flexes as a team. Note that you should have your players doing a lot of flexing in the locker room before ever coming out on the field. Use this team flex period more to build up enthusiasm than to truly stretch.

Call the team together and then have them break out to their offensive positions. After five minutes of drills, the whistle will blow and they move to their defensive positions.

The next whistle starts the team phase of pre-game warm-ups. First, call up the punt team. Place the ball on the one-foot line and have your punter punt out of your own end zone. The punter will kick it and your players will cover up the field and break down around the return man. Then a coach sets the ball on the 42-yard line and you "pooch" kick and cover it before it rolls into the end zone. Your PAT team lines up on the next whistle and your kicker gets three kicks. That completes the kicking game period of your pre-game warm-up. It is a part of the game that should not be overlooked if you are taking care of the *little things* that make a big difference.

At this point, have your starting defense huddle up. Get the scout team offense set up and run 8 to 12 of your opponent's plays against your defense. This time is your last chance for your defense to see those key plays that are a "must" to stop in the game. The aggression level will begin to rise at this point. Be careful that one of your more aggressive defenders doesn't wipe out one of your scout team players. Tackle during this period and wrap up, but do not tackle anybody to the ground. You will then switch to team offense and run 8 to 12 plays from your ready list while making personnel changes. With the last play, signal the team to leave the field.

Always leave the field running through the goal posts at your end. If you are at home, return to your locker room. If you are away, head to your "staging area" behind the end zone at your designated end of the field. Alert the team at home games that it is time to return to the field with the blaring of a song from your stereo system. The song will change over the years, but regardless of the song being played, you want it loud and rocking the locker room so you get that last ounce of adrenaline flowing. Meet them under the goalposts and remind them that "we are taking the field now—and we're not giving it back until this thing is over!" At home games, run to the 50-yard line and meet at your school emblem. Break the "Bruin" (refer to #77: Break the Bruin!), then hustle over to your bench. The game captains will go out for the ceremonial coin toss (always ask for a pre-game toss and instruct your captain to make the preferred call that you want—receive or defer if you win the toss) and call up the kicking team that is first on the field.

#77: Break the [Mascot]!

This idea is based on a ritual used by Emmitt Smith's Escambia High School (FL) coach, Dwight Thomas (*Bigger Faster Stronger Magazine*, March/April 1987). No matter where your team is, if they are together, you will not leave the area until you "break the [Mascot]." Whatever your school's mascot is, incorporate it into your "break."

Everyone comes up in a tight circle and they put their hands together reaching toward the middle. As head coach, always be in the middle of the team huddle. Everyone leans over and the players closest to you place their hands on yours down at knee level. You will slowly begin to raise your hands while everyone else begins to rise with their hands as they are moving up towards the sky. During this time, all of you will be chanting, "heeeeeeeey" and at the top, with everyone's hands in the air, you shout your school's name and mascot in unison as loud as you can.

Whether it is the lieutenants meeting for your weekly leadership meeting after Monday's practice, the seniors at your house for the goal planning session in June, or the team meeting together on the school emblem at the 50-yard line after a home game (win or lose), never leave any team gathering without "breaking the [Mascot]." It is a sign of team pride and solidarity.

#78: Staff/Player Communication During Games

Communication is an issue that you will probably have to address numerous times during your career. It seems that many assistant coaches have the impression that all the coaching is done when you leave the field on Thursday afternoon. Game night is a time to stand around and just enjoy the game like all of the spectators in the stands. The best coaches are the ones who are "game" coaches. These men see things happening in a game and make adjustments to take advantage of what they have diagnosed. Coaches need to observe and report to the coordinators what they are seeing as the game unfolds. If you are the offensive coordinator and play caller, you do not want anyone talking to you while you are on offense except to find out: one, down and distance; two, what yard line you are on; and three, which hash or middle of the field the ball is on. The spotters in the press box must be writing down the defensive front and coverage they see and what plays you call. Once the defense goes on the field, then you ask for input from your assistants. At halftime, a full analysis takes place and a second half mini game plan should be formulated. It is important that coaches remain active during the game. You should assign each of your assistants specific things to look for and be ready to report them in a timely fashion. If you have confidence in your assistants, you can request that they suggest a play that they think will be successful the next time your offense has the ball. If not, still look to them for input as far as what your opponent is doing.

One of the best sources of information in terms of what's happening on the field will come from your players themselves. Your offensive line coach should always have the linemen report to a designated site on your bench and, with a white board in hand, should get specific alignments and what particular defenders were doing on the previous series. It is not a time to berate and criticize, though getting a little fire started doesn't hurt. It is a time to gather information. If something has come down from the box as to what a particular player needs to change or correct, this point is the time to discuss it. Listen to your coaches and players.

A strong correlation exists between principles of warfare as presented in U.S. Army manuals and how you should conduct your "battle plan" on the game field. One of the key elements of successful warfare strategy is "information" or "intelligence." These bits of information are critical to an Army commander before and during a battle. The same thing is true for you. Gather "intelligence" to help you make good decisions during the heat of a game. The bottom line is: keep the lines of communication open during the game.

#79: Halftime Meetings

Many coaches fail to utilize that 20 minutes that you have to "regroup" at halftime. You should instruct your team to hustle off the field and get to your locker room or team area as quickly as possible. Your assistant coaches may be required to shepherd your players so they move quickly. Be sure to check with the head official before you leave the field to see what time he expects your team to be back on the sideline. Then you need to hurry onto the team area so you can greet your players as they are coming in.

First, meet in front of the team and give your evaluation of the first half. Always evaluate the team on two factors: one, their effort/enthusiasm; and two, their execution. It should be noted that the evaluation is always tempered by the level of competition of the opposing team. You can be playing well and be losing on the scoreboard because the team you are playing is outstanding. Exhort them to continue to do things the way they are doing them and good things will happen in the second half. You may be playing an inferior opponent and winning handily, but it's still possible to get upset with your team if they are not playing up to their capability. This talk should only take two or three minutes—remember, it's just a general overview of what happened in the first half. Then call for all of the coaches to meet you in the coach's office or away from the team so you can get feedback from them.

The first person you will want to hear from is your defensive coordinator. You want his observations of what he saw take place during the first half (you may add your evaluation or recommendation to what he saw). Ask him if there will be any changes and what he plans to do the second half. If you agree, send him and his defensive coaches out to meet with the defensive players; if you don't concur, make your recommendations and then send them out.

The next person you talk to is your quarterback coach. If you are the offensive coordinator and play caller, you want to hear what your quarterback coach thought of your first half on offense and how he thinks your quarterback played. Then ask your offensive line coach for his evaluation and any recommendations he suggests for the second half. Then send the quarterback coach out to get the quarterbacks and bring them back into the coach's office so you can talk with them. Then the receiver coach and running back have their say on what they saw the first half. Ask for recommendations as far as what all of them feel your offense needs to be running the second half. Your receiver coach should keep a chart of every play that you ran the first half and how efficient it was. He should compare that to your ready list (refer to #65: Game Plan and Ready List) to see if you were running the plays you designated as your "Big 5" and how well you ran them. Also discuss anyone's feelings that you should try something you haven't used yet. At that point, the offensive coaches leave if they need to talk to their position players. Make some notes on your ready list regarding recommendations for the second half. This staff conference should take about 8 to 10 minutes. Return to the team and tell them what you need to do the second half to be successful and exhort them to "play hard, play fast, and play to the last whistle." Then, go back out for the second half.

#80: Halftime Pep Talk

As previously stated, the wise coach should not be a big fan of spiking his players' emotional state just before or during a game. You want them focused, determined, and enthusiastic…but not out of control. Thus, your halftime pep talks don't have to be all that "peppy." Always speak with passion and know how to raise your voice to emphasize a point. Your halftime pep talk, however, is based more on what your players need to do the second half than trying to stir their emotions. To be an effective communicator, you must possess strong public-speaking skills. If you lack them, you should consider taking a course on motivational speaking. Your tone of voice, facial expressions, gestures, and the volume you use can easily elicit an emotional response in your listener if you know how to control those things.

#81: Halftime Warm-Ups

Teams often start off the third quarter playing poorly. Some people observe it as "being flat" to start the second half or describe it as "sleepwalking" through the third quarter. Sometimes, the intensity level of the players just doesn't produce the results that you want from your team as the second half gets under way.

This lack of intensity might be directly related to how your team takes the field to begin the second half, as illustrated by the following example. A coach noticed one night that his team came back on the field and they seemed to be "going through the motions" during their warm-ups in the end zone. He briskly strode down to where the team was, blew his whistle, and yelled, "Get 'em choppin'!" They all knew that they were going to be doing a few "up/downs" right there before the second half began. His team knew that those words were his signal to them that he was not pleased with the effort or level of intensity they were exhibiting.

During that halftime warm-up period, he proceeded to have them hit the ground six or seven times and then he called them up. He reprimanded them for their lackadaisical attitude and he let them know that if they continued it in the second half, they were going to pay for it. What a wake-up call. It was the hardest he'd ever seen them play in the second half of a game. At the Monday lieutenant's meeting they all agreed that the "wake-ups" needed to become a permanent part of their halftime warm-ups.

After having your team do a few old-fashioned calisthenics, blow your whistle, and tell them to "get 'em choppin'!" You only need to do three or four repetitions to wake them up and get their hearts pumping. It is an effective means of getting your team ready to play for the second half. Coaches will spend 30 to 45 minutes in pre-game getting their players properly warmed up and then fail to do so at halftime.

You and your players will also find it interesting to watch your opponents' faces as they pass you heading for their bench. You are in the end zone doing up/downs while they are walking back to their sideline. It will prove to be a real psychological boost for you when you point out to your team that you just demoralized your opponent by working so hard during halftime warm-ups. It is a tremendous source of team pride.

#82: Stand at Attention for the Alma Mater

If your team doesn't stand at attention for the alma mater, you should start to as a new team tradition for your program. Observe the coaches and players at the Army-Navy game standing at attention for each other's alma mater after the game, and you will see the impact it can have on school pride.

Explain to your band director what you want to do. Ask him to give your players and coaches time to conclude your handshake walk with your opponents and then watch you line up on the near hash mark in front of his band. Your players should remove their helmets and stand respectfully as the band plays your school's alma mater.

As the last line of the song plays, all of the players will raise their helmet over their heads and salute the band. It is a very poignant moment, particularly for your seniors, and will develop a lot of team and school pride. When the student body and fans see your team standing and facing the band as they play, don't be surprised if you see everyone else stop and do the same.

At the last home game that I coached, I joined the band. I asked the band director if I could be a member of the band when they played the alma mater. With some perplexity on her face, she agreed. When it was time for the band to perform after the game, I raced into the stands and grabbed the cymbals (did I mention that I do not play a musical instrument?) and waited until that moment in the last line of the song that calls for a big crash. I hit those big cymbals together with a resounding crash right on cue and the stadium went crazy. I'd do it every season at the last home game if I was still coaching.

#83: Post-Game Team Meeting

If you've been coaching for at least a couple of seasons, you have seen that it is very difficult to get 40 or 50 players into the locker room quick enough after a game to conduct a brief post-game meeting. Players are standing around talking to family and friends, some are being interviewed by the press or some media person, and others are just trying to be noticed.

Be sure that you meet with your team in the end zone for a brief meeting. This brief meeting is important to bring closure to the game. If you are home, line up, shake hands with your opponent, meet on the 50-yard line emblem, and "break the Bruin." By this time, a lot of the players' parents will have worked their way down to the field and you should not have a problem with them standing off to the side while you talk with your players. It is important to "temper" what you say, in terms of being critical of your team, if you have parents standing within earshot.

Talk to the players about their effort and execution, as you did at halftime. If an individual really has an outstanding night, you can recognize him and have the team (and parents) give him a big round of applause. This moment can be that "unsung hero" recognition time you want. It might be your punter who kept you in the game with four booming punts in the second half. Recognize him and the punt snapper for a job well done right there on the field after the game. Any opportunity you can find to promote goodwill with the parents nearby is time well spent.

#84: Rain-Out/Make-Up Games

If it is game day and it is raining and you are the home team, do everything possible to convince the athletic director and your principal that you want to play that night. If at all feasible, you need to stay consistent in your preparation. It can be difficult to face your players at 4 p.m. on Friday afternoon and tell them that their game is going to be postponed.

If a game is postponed, have a routine that you have established so veterans will know that you are going to plan B—business as usual. Get your lieutenants to move around the locker room and point out to your rookies in particular that "they (your opponent) can run but they can't hide! They're just postponing the inevitable. They'll just have to face us tomorrow instead of tonight." It's all part of the mind game that you must play to keep high school kids focused and positive in their attitude.

Your "postponement routine" should include sending the team home after a short meeting announcing the cancellation and watching 15 to 20 minutes of the opponent's scout video. If your staff checks on the players to be sure they aren't out late on Thursday night when you have a Friday game, then have them check on the players again on Friday night if the game has been rescheduled for Saturday. If you don't check on them on Thursday night, then don't check on them on Friday night. Remind the players that if they don't have any more respect for your team than to stay out late on the night before a game, then they don't deserve to win. The manner in which you address your players regarding staying out late is something that you will have to decide based on how much you trust them to have a free Friday night. You may feel that you need your coaches to call every player by 10 p.m. to let them know that someone will be checking, however, they can leave and go out at 11 p.m. as easily as they can go out at 8 p.m.

You should always have a walk-through practice on Saturday morning. This practice is to get the players to school by 9:30 a.m. to walk through a brief review of your game plans and to watch more game video, which will start the re-focus process for that evening's make-up game. Have them report to the stadium at your regular time as if it were a Friday afternoon game except you will tell them to eat before they report. A lot of players will go to a local restaurant and eat a pre-game meal together. Tell them to watch some college football, get off their feet, rehydrate, and get themselves mentally prepared to play even better than they would have played the previous night. If you are the visitor, which means the other team made the decision to postpone the game, use the fact that they canceled as a positive motivator. Blame the opponent for ruining the players' weekend. Tell your team that they get a chance to see what it's like to play at a time that colleges normally play. Come up with anything that you can to stir them up emotionally. At 4 p.m., everyone reports to the locker room and you begin (again) your pre-game ritual just like you do on Friday.

7

Parent/Community Relations

If a high school coach is going to build a program that is successful for the long haul, he has to focus on and draw into his camp three important components of his school's community: the parents, the youth league coaches, and the local business owners. First and foremost, however, are the players' parents. I always make it clear to the parents that I know that they are giving me responsibility for their most precious possession— their son. Many moms are fearful of letting their sons play football, so you need to help them to see that you are looking out for their son's best interest, not only on the field but in the classroom and at home. Winning helps to gain the respect of your parents, but it will be well-known throughout your school and community if you are the type of football coach who respects his players as young men as well as athletes.

#85: Pre-Season Letter to Parents

Toward the end of July each year, mail a letter to the players informing them about physicals, pre-season practice times, and inviting them to the pre-season player/parent orientation meeting. In that envelope you will also include a letter to the parents, which is an invitation to the orientation meeting as well as an explanation of what you hope to gain through working together to achieve the "double win," which means that you want their son to be successful both on *and* off the field. Tell the parents and/or guardians about how you want to work with them to achieve this success.

The letter should include some information on how they can be better "football parents." Talk about how they can help make the season the best possible experience for their whole family. This letter lays the groundwork for what you will hope to be a positive and rewarding relationship between you as the coach and the players' families. Figure 7-1 provides a sample parents' letter.

Dear football parent,

I would like to share some ideas with you that will help make this football season a rewarding experience for you and your son and leave a lot of positive memories for your family.

- Make sure that your son knows, win or lose, that you love him. Be the person in his life he can always look to for support.
- Try to be completely honest with yourself about your son's athletic capability, his competitive attitude, his sportsmanship, and his level of skills.
- Be helpful, but don't coach your son on Saturday morning or at the supper table after practice. Think about how tough it would be on him to be continually inundated with advice, pep talks, and criticism.
- Teach your son to enjoy the thrill of competition, to be constantly working to improve his skills, to take physical bumps, and come back for more. Don't tell him that "winning doesn't count" because it does—and he knows it. Instead, help him to develop a healthy competitive attitude, a "feel" for competing, for trying hard, and for having a good time.
- Try not to live your life through your son. You've lost at some time in life as well as won. You've been frightened and you've backed off at times. Sure, he's an extension of you, but don't assume he feels the same way you did, wants the same things, or has the same attitude as you.
- Don't push him in the direction that gives you the most satisfaction. Don't compete with his coaches. A coach may become a hero to your son for a while—someone

---

Figure 7-1. Sample parents' letter

who can do no wrong—and you may find that hard to take. At the same time, don't automatically side with your son against his coaches. Try to help him understand the necessity for discipline, rules, and regulations.

- Don't compare your son to other players on the team—at least not within the other players' hearing. Don't lie to your son about his capabilities as a player or, if you are overly protective, you can perpetuate the problem.
- Get to know the coaches. Coaches can be influential and you should know the values of each coach. At our high school, we will never consciously make a decision that hurts your son. We are here to help, challenge, encourage, and motivate your son to be the best he can be in all phases of his life.
- Remember that children tend to exaggerate. Temper your reactions to stories he brings home about how he was praised or criticized. Don't criticize him for exaggerating, but don't overreact to the stories he tells. If you have concerns, contact the coach for verification.
- Teach your son the meaning of courage. Everyone is frightened about something. Courage isn't the absence of fear—it's learning to perform in spite of fear. Courage isn't getting rid of fear—it's overcoming it.
- Winning is an important goal. However, winning at all costs is foolish.
- Remember that game officials are necessary. Don't overreact to their calls. The players have rules and guidelines to follow regarding authority on the field. Teach your son to respect authority and to play by the rules.

I have given a lot of advice in this letter about *teaching* your son. Please don't think that because your son is a teen that he doesn't still need to learn from you. Continue to emphasize the values that you have taught him since he was young. He's still maturing and needs to have these important values reinforced. As his coaches, we will also continue to instill these values. We want to work *with* you to help him grow into a productive, successful young adult. We want to support you in this venture. Please let us know how we can help you.

I have had several parents of players from other schools that have complimented you (our football parents) on your spirit, your support of our team, and your sportsmanship, which are qualities that I am very proud of when I think of our football family. You should also be proud of these attributes.

Sincerely,
Lew Johnston
Head Football Coach

Figure 7-1. Sample parents' letter (cont.)

#86: Team Newsletter

Keeping with the theme of "communication," a good way to keep parents informed is to send home a newsletter every week. If you have a team website, you can post all the announcements there. If you do not have anyone who can run a website for you, you can send the parents an e-mail or hard-copy newsletter with information that they will want to know. Weekly award winners, head coach's analysis of the game, a preview of the upcoming opponent, and announcements concerning times of events are all items that keep parents informed and less likely to call the head coach to ask questions.

During the off-season, you can send home a newsletter once a month, which will keep the parents in the loop during the winter and spring and also keep the football program's activities in the forefront of the players' and parents' minds. A team newsletter is a great way to keep the players' families informed.

#87: Orientation Meeting Information

Make it a requirement for parents to attend the pre-season orientation meeting. If the players want to start practice on the first day, their parents must attend. Make the orientation meeting mandatory for all the players as well. Tell them that the meeting is considered a practice and if they fail to attend they will do extra conditioning after the first on-field practice.

At this meeting, review your player policies (Figure 7-2) in detail and have the players and parents sign the policy agreement sheet that is included on the last page of the policies packet. If a problem comes up during the season, refer to the player policy sheet to remind parents how you deal with the issue in your program.

You should also discuss how parents can get involved in your program. Some coaches are not advocates of parent booster clubs because the parents start thinking they are entitled to special treatment since they donate money and time to the program. Look for creative ways to get your parents involved in your program without allowing them to think that they are somehow putting you in their debt. Offer your parents opportunities to run the pre-season family picnic (refer to #50: Team/Family Picnic), organize and present the season-end banquet (refer to #90: Post-Season Team Banquet), be a part of the field maintenance crew (refer to #92: Field Maintenance Crew), or, perhaps the most helpful, be a part of the paint crew (refer to #89: Paint Crew).

During the pre-season meeting, always make two things abundantly clear to the parents. First, you are always available to talk to them about their concerns. You should stipulate, however, that they are to call the school to make an appointment or to talk on the phone when it's convenient for you. Under no circumstances should you allow yourself to be "accosted" by an upset parent after a game or practice. Second, let the parents know that they are giving you responsibility to care for their sons. You need to emphasize that you will treat their sons as you would treat your own if he played for your team.

You should also emphasize to parents that you cannot get their son a college scholarship, which is a huge misconception among many parents. Explain that the decision as to who is offered a scholarship is strictly up to the college coaches. Share with them that you will work as hard as you can to get their son's name to colleges, make videos, and write recommendations, but you do not have the power nor influence to get a scholarship for their son. Once they understand this, you will have fewer problems with parents.

Football Player Policies

The guidelines we set down for everyone to follow are designed to help you as an individual, promote *team unity*, and maintain discipline. After reviewing the policies, detach the back page, sign it, and return it to Coach Johnston before you leave tonight.

To compete for our team, you must follow the policies presented below. Any infraction of these policies will lead to disciplinary action or even removal from the team.

- *Dishonesty*. Dishonesty will NOT be tolerated. Lying to a coach, cheating, or stealing from someone affiliated with the team is inexcusable. It will result in benching, disciplinary action (extra conditioning) or possible dismissal from the team.

- *Be at practice*. Practices are our chief means of preparing for our games. If you want to play, you *must* attend all practices.

  ✓ *Unexcused absences* are any absence where a coach is not contacted prior to the start of practice as to your whereabouts by the player or his parents (i.e., a phone call or your name on the absentee list during school and/or non-approval by Coach Johnston to miss). For each unexcused absence, it will cost you 400 yards of drills at the end of the next practice you attend. If the unexcused absence occurs during game week, it will also mean benching for at least a quarter. If you have two unexcused absences in one game week, you will be suspended from playing that week and will have to win back your position the following week.

  ✓ *Excused absences* are those approved by the head coach prior to the beginning of practice. If you are absent from school due to illness, you may attend practice that day but you may not participate. Any *excused* absence from practice (illness or injury, etc.) will result in the coach's decision as to whether you will start on Friday. You will be required to make up all conditioning you miss while you are absent. If you are injured, see guideline regarding injuries and attending practice.

  ✓ *Late arrivals*: Anyone desiring to come out late for the team will first be evaluated by the coaching staff to determine if the reason for coming out late is valid. If approved, he must first spend five days without full pads and make up all conditioning before being allowed contact or playing time.

  ✓ *Excessive absences (five)* from school and/or practice will require a conference with your parents and the coach to discuss the problem. Suspension or dismissal from the team will be considered at that time.

- *Be on time*. In fact, be *early*. We will stick to our practice schedule as long as we get started on time. Being late to practice will cost you extra conditioning for as many minutes as you are late at the beginning of practice.

- *No profanity*. By players or coaches. It's a sign of no self-discipline and a limited vocabulary, plus I find it offensive. Anyone caught will drop for 15 push-ups (personal foul penalty). Repeated violations will result in disciplinary action after practice.

- *Sportsmanship*. We will treat our teammates with respect at all times. The fastest way to break down team unity is to ridicule a teammate. We are here to encourage and build each other up—not tear down. Rookies are *not* second-class citizens. If anything, they need more encouragement from teammates.

Figure 7-2. Sample player policy sheet

- ✓ We will treat our managers and trainers with the same respect as teammates. They work very hard in a (mostly) thankless job. Let them know you appreciate what they do.
- ✓ During games, we will conduct ourselves in a manner that brings pride to our school and our family. In fact, wherever we wear our school colors, we represent our high school and our football team. Every action that we take reflects on the team as a whole. We are role models in the community and people are watching us.
- ✓ We will respect our opponents and the officials before, during, and after the game. We will play hard, but we will play clean and by the rules. Make your opponent *fear* you and *respect* you. We will create a good impression with the officials by not complaining about their calls.
- ✓ If a fight breaks out on the field during a game, no one (players or coaches) may enter the field. If you are near the fight, get away from it—fast. The video will continue to film and anyone viewed being involved in the fight will be automatically suspended for the next two games. You'll also have to visit with me personally after practice for several days to remind you about the importance of sportsmanship. Remember our walk-away drill.

- *Lettering*. A varsity football letter is something to be earned by those who contribute on the field during games. To earn a varsity letter in football, a player must appear in at least seven games during the course of the season. An appearance is counted as at least one play during the game.
- *Player cuts*. We will have at least one pre-season cut to get to a workable number of 40 to 50 varsity players. Making the team will be based on two general criteria: one, possessing the skills to make a contribution to the team's success; and two, possessing a positive attitude and good work habits. We will cut anyone (*at any point during the season*) if the coaches feel that a player is failing to exhibit either of these criteria.
- *Alcohol, drugs, and tobacco products*. These substances have no business being used by anyone—let alone athletes trying to perform at peak levels for 13 to 16 weeks. If you care about yourself and your team, you'll stay away from these things. If reported, we'll investigate. If caught, punishment will be severe. Being caught using drugs or alcohol will result in at least a two-game suspension. The maximum penalty is dismissal from the team and enrollment in a drug/alcohol counseling program. Use of tobacco products will result in a disciplinary period after practice for three days. Repeat offenders can and will be suspended. This is a *pride* factor and we take it very seriously.
- *Closed practices*. For safety's sake and to keep our players' attention on practice, we ask all family and friends to stay a good distance back from our practice field if they desire to watch. The bleachers on the softball field are a good vantage point. Also, no one except for team members is allowed in our locker room unless invited by a staff member. Female managers and trainers will not be allowed in the locker room when players are changing clothes.
- *Parent/player and coach conferences*. If you or your parents feel the need to discuss a concern with a coach, contact Coach Johnston during the school day to make an appointment. No conferences will be allowed before, during, or just after a practice or game. We want to communicate with you. Please make it at an appropriate time.
- *Injuries*. Report all injuries to the head trainer. If the trainer is not available, contact a coach. The trainer can evaluate and treat your problem. The trainers' job is to get you back on the

Figure 7-2. Sample player policy sheet (cont.)

field as soon as it is prudent. All decisions concerning permission to return to practice following an injury come from our medical staff. Parents: please try to see our team doctor before you take your son to your family doctor. Our medical staff is excellent and they are trained in dealing with sports injuries. *Note*: If you are *injured*, you are required to attend all practices. An injured player will dress in football practice gear and be on the practice field. You will be under the supervision of the training staff and take part in whatever activity is deemed appropriate for you. As long as you attend *all* practices *and* participate in at least Thursday's practice, you may play that week, but you may not necessarily start or play the whole game.

- *Equipment*. Take care of your equipment. Every piece of equipment issued to you is the property of our school. If you lose it or destroy it, it is you or your parents' responsibility to pay to replace it. If you look sharp— you play sharp. We outfit you in the best equipment available. Take pride in what you wear. On a weekly basis, check your equipment. If it is broken, get it repaired. If it needs replacing, see a coach. Proper equipment is a necessary part of your safety. Wash your clothing as least once a week (more frequent when it's hot). Follow the game uniform guidelines stipulated by Coach Johnston.

- *Locker room*. No horse-play in the varsity or JV locker room. Keep your locker and the area around it clean and clear of debris. Put *all* equipment inside your locker and lock the door every day. Failure to follow these procedures will result in punishment and loss of locker room privileges. The training room is part of the varsity locker room. You will abide by what the trainer tells you to do. Our head trainer has the same authority as a coach and you will respect that authority.

- *Leadership*. Our football team is unique in that we count on more than just two or three captains to provide leadership. Our system of selecting lieutenants has been very effective. Virtually everyone on the team has an opportunity to be evaluated as a potential lieutenant. Our cadre of leaders is nominated by every player and coach with the final selection being made by the head coach. Lieutenants are selected after a tryout/observation period during the pre-season. Our lieutenants are expected to carry out our team philosophy of *Unity, Pride, and Total Effort* everyday. Failure to uphold these ideals can and will result in demotion. Also, any player who, during the course of the season, begins to exhibit the qualities expected in our leaders can receive a battlefield promotion. It is the rest of the team's responsibility to respect our lieutenants and follow their good example.

- *Attitude*. Attitude is everything. We want football players who are enthusiastic and positive in nature. A positive mental attitude is perhaps the single, most important attribute for an athlete. Each of us is a key element in the success of our team. Every player must know his role and work hard to be the best he can be in that role—whether he's a two-way starter or a rookie still trying to earn some playing time by working hard against the starters in practice every day. Every one of us needs to adopt our slogan of: BIG *TEAM*, little *me*. If all of us (players, coaches, parents, managers, and trainers) will strive to incorporate our team philosophy of unity, pride, and total effort every day of the season, we will have a great year.

Lew Johnston
Head Football Coach

Figure 7-2. Sample player policy sheet (cont.)

Football Player Policy Agreement

I have had the player policies explained to me and I understand their importance. By signing this paper, I am agreeing to uphold the policies set forth by the coaches. I also understand that failure to abide by these policies can result in disciplinary action taken against me, including suspension or dismissal from the team.

_____   _____

Player's signature   Date

_____

Player's printed name

_____   _____

Parent's signature   Date

_____

Parent's printed name

Figure 7-2. Sample player policy sheet (cont.)

#88: Philosophy and Mission Statement

It is important that any head coach *know* why he is coaching and what he is trying to accomplish in his program. Just as important is defining *how* he is going to achieve these goals. The crux of a coaching philosophy is knowing how and what you want to achieve. You need to sit down and decide one, what you want to achieve, and two, how you are going to achieve it. You need to remember that coaching in high school is a lot more than just winning on Friday night. If you are not going to teach values and character to these young men, you are going to fail them. Go for the "double win." You should want them to be successful on *and* off the field. You have expectations and you must be sure that your players (and coaches) adhere to them. Choose your battles, but where you stick your flag in the ground is where you've chosen to defend your philosophy. Stand and fight for what you believe in. Figure 7-3 provides a sample of a mission statement.

Mission Statement

Our *mission* (our purpose) is to take our athletes where they cannot take themselves. This goal will ultimately lead us to becoming a great football team—defined as one that is composed of individuals who *consistently* perform up to and beyond their limits as athletes, students, and people.
- We will foster an environment that teaches young men to:
  - ✓ Relentlessly pursue and win the district championship, the regional championship and the state championship
  - ✓ Appreciate and respect *every* member of our football program
  - ✓ Achieve an exemplary level of leadership and academic success.
- Our mission is based on the values of *unity, pride,* and *total effort.*
- We believe in *loyalty, team chemistry, selflessness,* and *honesty.*
- We embrace a commitment to *excellence, confidence, humility, positive attitude,* and *strength of character.*
- We teach *overcoming adversity, establishing priorities, goal setting, persistence,* and *giving 100 percent all the time.*

Lew Johnston
Head Football Coach

Figure 7-3. Sample mission statement

#89: Paint Crew

If your school district does not have maintenance employees who are responsible for having your stadium ready for home games, then you need to consider inviting your parents to take charge of this important activity. You can solicit parent support by letting a responsible and willing parent take charge of painting the field for your home games. Supply him with a couple of industrial-size paint sprayers. He will get some other parents to commit to be there every Wednesday and Thursday, and this group will take a lot of pride in how the lines on the field look. For homecoming week, buy them some extra paint and let them decorate the end zones. A favorite is the classic University of Tennessee checkerboard design in your school colors. Your field will be the envy of your whole district.

If you can hand this chore off to parents who care about how your game field will look and are vested in your program, you can go home after practice on Thursday night, instead of staying late with your coaches to paint the field. Buy the members of the paint crew t-shirts that recognize who they are. Get your athletic director to give them free admission to all home games and ask the PA announcer to call their names and give them a big "thank you" each week during the game. You need to let the paint crew know that you appreciate what they are doing for you.

#90: Post-Season Team Banquet

Arrange for your parents to spearhead your team banquet. Your players and parents will expect to be in charge of this event because it is the way that community league teams conduct their season-ending banquets. Food should be provided by the parents, however, if there are funds available, you can have it catered. Decorate the school cafeteria and hold your banquet there. The parents will arrange for everything and will do a great job because it is for their sons.

After eating, present a season highlight video with music, which is a great way to set the tone for the rest of the evening's events. Present the players with their letters and awards. As you call each individual player up to receive his award, make sure to say something positive about every player who made it through the entire season. Recognition is a tremendous motivator for athletes. Choose your words carefully. Take some notes beforehand, if you need to, and be sure that you do not leave out a single player. Everything that you say must be to encourage and motivate. Do not embarrass or degrade any child—especially with parents in attendance. You can talk about what each player accomplished during the season and how much you are counting on him for next year, which is another great motivational tool.

Guest speakers are nice but their speeches take up time that should be afforded to the players. If you can get a recognized coach or player to come, explain to him that he can only have 7 to 10 minutes. If you do not choose to have a guest speaker, explain to your parents that you do not want one because you want as much time devoted to their sons as possible.

Present your Golden [Mascot] award last (refer to #20: Golden [Mascot] Club). These awards are presented to the one or two players whom you and your staff feel went above and beyond the call of duty throughout the season. Then, conclude the night's activities by calling your seniors to come forward and receive a standing ovation. The end of the season is a time to forget the mistakes and problems and focus on the positive. Whether that group of seniors did a great job of leading or not, you can still thank them for all that they did for you during the past season. Your underclassmen will be out there watching and taking in everything that you say and do.

#91: College Recruiting Meetings

Be aware that 99 percent of your players, from your star to your benchwarmer, dream of playing college football. At some point, you will have to explain to that 5'9" 220-pound second-string lineman that he is just not big enough to play for Ohio State or Florida—even if those are his "dream schools."

For the player who you recognize early in his career really has the ability to play Division 1A football, you should set up a meeting with his parents after his sophomore season. This meeting should be private, with just the parents, the player, and you in attendance. It is an opportunity to sit down face-to-face and talk about their son's future in football. You will want to bring a copy of the player's transcript so you can review his grades and a copy of the NCAA Clearinghouse's list of accepted core courses taught at your school. Lay out a two-year plan of what classes he should take and what grades he needs to earn to meet minimum eligibility requirements. Many parents have no knowledge of the Clearinghouse or anything about college recruiting; direct them to https://web1.ncaa.org/eligibilitycenter/general/index_general.html where they can download the Division I and II Worksheet. If the recruiting process takes off, show the parents that you will be their ambassador. It is crucial to explain to them that you as the coach see potential in their young sophomore to be a college recruit but that the player needs to take care of a lot of things both academically and athletically before the dream of a college scholarship becomes a reality.

With the proliferation of recruiting websites and combines, players are getting bombarded with information overload at a much earlier age than ever before. As a coach who cares about his players, it behooves you to meet with these parents and explain the recruiting process. Direct them to the NCAA Clearinghouse website as a great resource for information about the whole recruiting process. Always let them know that you are right there to help them with any questions or concerns they might have as this process unfolds. One thing you must always emphasize is that you cannot "get" their son a scholarship. Make sure that they understand that you will make phone calls, write recommendations, and send game video, but you as the high school coach do not have the power nor influence to get their son a scholarship. The colleges know what they are looking for and there are times that you will have to "agree to disagree" with the college recruiter about how the college evaluates one of your players. In the end, it is the college coach who decides who they recruit. Figure 7-4 provides a list of things to do to prepare for being recruited to play college football.

Recruiting Preparation List

- *Keep your grades up.* You need to have a 2.0 GPA in your *academic* classes for the college recruiters to even take an initial interest in you. The higher your *core* GPA, the lower your SAT/ACT score has to be.
- *Take the PSAT.* October is the only month the PSAT is offered, so take it in the fall of your junior year. Take it your sophomore year too—it is for practice only.
- *Do some things to enhance your skills.* Obviously, your athletic skills are in a lot of ways god-given natural ability, but there are some things you can do to enhance those skills:
  - ✓ Get involved in the weight-lifting program as early as possible in your high school career.
  - ✓ Run track or do speed and agility training—anything to improve your 40-yard-dash time.
  - ✓ Take a weight supplement. To gain weight, you have to put more "good" calories into your body per day than you burn up. Protein supplements (without creatine) have shown themselves to work if you are willing to take them on a daily basis for three-to-six months.
- *Plan to attend football camps at colleges that you are interested in.* It's a chance for their coaches to see you work out and your opportunity to visit the campus and see their football facilities.
- *Give a total effort on every play that you are on the field—whether it's the practice field or the game field.* College coaches are looking for the player whose motor runs in overdrive for every snap. Run hard every play—because the "eye in the sky" (video camera) does not lie.
- *Be coachable.* When the college recruiter interviews any member of your coaching staff, be sure that there are positive things to report about your work habits and your attitude.
- *Stay out of trouble in school.* If you develop a bad reputation with the high school faculty and administrators, the college recruiters will find out about it. That is a sure-fire way to get lowered down the list that recruiters compile.

Figure 7-4. Sample recruiting preparation list

#92: Field Maintenance Crew

Organize a paint crew (refer to #89: Paint Crew) but also consider forming a field maintenance crew. Make this parent group responsible for keeping your game field and practice field mowed and manicured. They will coordinate schedules with the paint crew. Between the two parent groups, your game field will be the showplace in your entire area.

#93: Community League/Middle School Contacts

The lifeblood of any high school program is the feeder schools or community league that sends its players on to the high school. If you don't cultivate your relationship with these people, you will hurt your chances for long-term success.

Several activities exist that can be used to let those feeder programs know that they are important to you. Let them know that you want to help in any way that you can to make them successful also. The first thing you should do is to conduct a coach's clinic for all community-league coaches. Plan to meet for three nights in July to go over offense, defense, kicking game, and fundamentals. Suggest that the community league and junior high coaches adopt your offensive and defensive systems and terminology. Let them know that you are available to answer questions throughout the season.

Conduct a football camp for the younger players. Varsity athletes can earn community-service hours for helping with your camp. If it is feasible, this can also be a means of you supplementing your summer income by charging a fee for each player who attends.

It is extremely important is to be "seen" by the younger players. Make it a point to stop by your feeder schools during their pre-season and observe them practicing. Their coach will usually allow you to call players together to introduce yourself, and allow you a few minutes to talk to the team. Let them know that you will be watching them as their season progresses and you are looking forward to working with them when they get to high school. Always talk about grades and character as the two most important things they should be concentrating on. Then, if their game time allows it, show up for their games. You want to be seen out in the community supporting these programs.

8

Character-Building Exercises

As much as any coach enjoys the success of coaching and the personal accolades that come with that success, if you do not enjoy being around teenagers and helping kids, you are coaching for the wrong reasons. For many players, their coach is their hero. You should teach your players how to be successful on and off the field. Demonstrate to your players every day that you care about them as individuals, not just as football players. Teach them about life as well as football. Talk to your players about "character" and do *little things* to help develop their character. Your responsibilities go beyond what happens on the playing field. Many teenage boys don't have a positive male role model in their life. You, as the football coach, must carry the load.

#94: Team-Building Exercises

Involve your players in one of these exercises every day after lunch during your pre-season camp. Then, as your season progresses, have your team do one occasionally on Monday or Thursday to re-emphasize the importance of team unity and pride.

You can find lists of these activities in books and by searching on the Internet. Some are designed as "ice breakers," some build trust in others, and some simply challenge the individual to look inside himself. One of the best exercises you can do is to allow your players to perform skits that typify a "day in the life of a (your school) football player." These skits are best done on the last day of camp after the team has been through a hard week of practice on the field as well as four days of bonding through team building exercises. The players have the chance to mimic the coaches and it is really funny to see them act out how they view you and your staff. The rules are that they have to keep it clean and nobody is allowed to humiliate anyone during the performance. It should be done in the sprit of good fun. Your kids will love it. Be prepared to be mimicked by one of your players. It is amazing how much they "see" by being around you every day.

For these exercises to be effective, you have to create "teachable moments." Some of these exercises cause the players to search within themselves. You will see some strong emotional responses during and after the exercise is completed. Be prepared to use this time to teach your players a lesson that ties into your mission statement (refer to #87: Philosophy and Mission Statement). You should always "process" what the kids see and feel after the activity is completed. It can be a special time when your players share some real insights into who they are and what is going on in their lives. It is a tremendous opportunity to build team unity.

#95: Word of the Week

It is important that you are big on building character in your student athletes. Each week, select a character trait that you feel all of your players should learn more about and emulate in their lives. Make it the focal point of all of your talks to the team throughout that week.

Have a special place in your locker room where you can start a list of "words of the week." As each week goes by, add another word just below the previous one. You want everyone to be able to see every word you have selected as your season progresses. Make sure you point out the new word to the team during your pre-practice meeting on Monday. At the end of every practice, when you call the team together to give them an evaluation of how you think the day went and talk about what you are building toward for the game on Friday, incorporate your "word of the week" into your comments. At the ceremony (refer to #62: Ceremony) on Thursday, the word should be the focal point of your pre-game pep talk. Present this key character trait to your players as often as possible, and then refer back to it later in the season when the opportunity presents itself. Drive home your point with inspirational stories, quotes, and handouts such as the one shown in Figure 8-1. The more your players hear your word of the week, the better they'll remember it.

By emphasizing such things as excellence, perseverance, respect, and teamwork, you are instilling positive character traits in your players' personalities. Show the players that these traits will help them be successful on the field Friday night and throughout their lives.

The Four E's of Excellence

The four "e's" in the word *excellence* each represent a character trait that is necessary to aspire to if a person wants to achieve *excellence*.

- *Education*: You will never achieve excellence if you do not learn as much as you can about the subject or activity that you desire to be excellent in. Being a lifelong learner is critical.
- *Execution*: Once you have educated yourself, you must apply what you have learned.
- *Effort*: You must put forth maximum effort on a consistent basis in order to achieve excellence in whatever you undertake.
- *Enthusiasm*: In his book *The Art of Public Speaking*, Ralph Waldo Emerson wrote, "Nothing great was ever achieved without enthusiasm." Enthusiasm is contagious; it's like a spark that gets a fire burning. An enthusiastic attitude makes it easier to give maximum effort.

The Four "E's" of Excellence are all interrelated. Each one builds on the next, allowing you to achieve *excellence*.

Figure 8-1. The Four E's of Excellence

#96: Team Chaplain

If it's appropriate for your situation, you can ask a local pastor if he would be your unofficial team chaplain. Let him know that he is welcome to visit your team during the week by dropping by on the practice field or just hanging out with the team in the locker room. A Young Life area director or a youth pastor at a church in your community would probably be very excited to help you out in this capacity.

On game days, set aside 10 minutes for a time of devotion and prayer. You can invite any player who would like to participate to grab a chair, leave the locker room (so those who do not want to participate do not feel they are being kicked out of their locker room), and join you and the chaplain under the bleachers or in the weight room for prayer. Ask your chaplain to be very cognizant of time, since you are on a tight schedule. He should give a five- to seven-minute exhortation utilizing a Bible verse to illustrate how your Word of the Week (refer to #95: Word of the Week) helps in their Christian walk. Then have a student-led prayer time. Building up your players spiritually, as well as physically and mentally, is important for them to become well-rounded young men.

#97: Inspirational Stories

For a pep talk to have the desired effect on your players, it is important to arouse their emotions. Sales trainers will tell you that if you want to make a sale you have to appeal to the potential buyer on an emotional level. The same holds true if you are trying to inspire your players.

When you speak to your players you need to be organized. You could even consider taking a public speaking class. One of the elements of being an effective coach and motivator is being an effective public speaker. Anyone who gives a speech to a group needs to have his introduction, body, and conclusion prepared ahead of time.

Make a point of looking for inspirational stories that you can weave into your talks. Don't underestimate the power of a sad story or a story of someone who overcame insurmountable odds to stir your audience's emotions. It is important to develop a file of stories and keep them by topics: endurance, trust, teamwork, etc. are subject headings that you should file stories under so you can refer to them quickly when you need a story. Books are available for purchase, which are specifically designed to provide public speakers with inspirational stories. Just like the parables in the Bible, a good story will capture the interest of the audience and elicit an emotional response.

#98: Use of Movie Clips

Keeping in tune with the impact that visual aids have on people's emotional state, one of the most effective ways to emphasize a point with your team is to show a clip from a popular movie. One movie clip, for instance, that you should use numerous times is a scene from *Sister Act II*. In it, the nun character that Whoopee Goldberg is playing confronts her high school chorus class and tells them, "It's a new day. If you want to be somebody, if you want to go somewhere, then you'd better wake up and pay attention." This quote can become your team slogan for an entire season. At the conclusion of team meetings, you should remind your players of the importance of "waking up and paying attention" to what their coaches are trying to teach them.

Kids watch a lot of movies. If you are creative, you can find a scene from a popular movie that will illustrate a key point you are trying to make. A visual cue can be a strong motivator for your players. Insert the clip at the appropriate time in your talk to *show* the players what you are trying to say. The old saying is true: "a picture is worth a 1000 words."

Note: Be sure to check on copyright laws before you download a segment of a movie. The length of the segment is also a factor to be considered. Check with your school's computer specialist for the latest information.

9

Fundraising Projects

Fundraisers are the scourge of high school athletics. Yet, they are necessary if a coach wants to purchase the equipment he needs to have a successful program. This chapter presents some "easy" suggestions of ways to do fundraising. I define "easy" as fast—get it done in one or two days, collect the money, and it's over. Explain to your team that you are having the fundraiser to help them and that they will be rewarded by participating. All types of groups use fundraising activities, however, there are people in your community who are willing to donate to a good cause, such as the local football team, if you present the activity in a polite manner.

#99: Donut Sale

You can do an annual donut sale on the first Saturday of pre-season practice, which is when you will have the maximum number of players available to deliver donuts in your community. Contact a local donut store to make arrangements. Krispy Kreme, for example, is set up to deal with fundraising events and they will be very helpful. The key to this fundraiser is to do everything as *pre-sale*, which makes the task easy and profitable. The players collect the money for the boxes of donuts *before* the donuts are delivered. Each player has four days to turn the money in to the coach responsible for collecting the money, in order for the donuts to be delivered on Saturday. You will pick up your donuts early Saturday morning and bring them to your stadium. Have a designated time for your players and parents to pick up their orders. Since you pre-sold the boxes, all the player has to do is deliver them.

Encourage each player to sell a dozen boxes of donuts. Thus, if you charge $5.00 a box, you can expect $60.00 from every player. The "carrot" to use that provides the incentive to sell all 12 boxes is to tell your players that for every box of donuts they sell, they get out of one sprint in conditioning that Saturday *after* practice, which is the one day that you will save conditioning until the end. It will be the first day in full pads and it may be hot, so it can be one of the hardest workouts of your entire pre-season. The traditional conditioning for that day is 12 110-yard sprints with full gear on. Remind them that it's not punishment if they have to run because it's on the schedule to condition at the end of practice that particular day. But if they would like to get out of running, they just need to sell the donuts. You will find that you will have amazing sales results. Each kid who participates will sell all 12 boxes in order to get out of running.

#100: Penny-a-Pound Lift-a-Thon

This fundraiser should be held in conjunction with your Superstars Competition in June (refer to #21: Superstars Competition). It will be part of your "testing" at the end of your off-season weight-lifting program. The players get pledges from parents, neighbors, teachers, and/or friends to sponsor them in a lifting contest. The person pledges to give the player a penny for each pound he lifts in your four core lifts: bench, power clean, squat, and push press. Thus, if a player lifts a combined weight of 1,000 pounds, the pledger will donate $10.00 to that player. Encourage each player to get at least 25 pledges. When the lifting is completed, the players collect the money and turn in their donations.

You can use monetary prizes as a reward. For example, if a player turns in $50.00, you can give him $5.00 back. If he turns in $100.00, give him $10 back. It's money in their pocket, so they will be willing to get out there and get those pledges.

#101: Sale of Team T-Shirts and Used Equipment

Make every t-shirt you sell to players, parents, and fans a fundraiser. Print up a team t-shirt for each season with the year of that particular season screen-printed on the front, which will designate it as a commemorative keepsake for that season. Then, offer it for sale to players, parents, and their families. When you win championships, print up a shirt and sell it around school and in the community. If you sell at least 200 shirts with a $5 dollar profit, you've got $500 to $1000 dollars with little or no work.

You can sell a school weightlifting t-shirt during the off-season. The younger players who come over from the middle schools will love them. They will go back to their school the next day with a high school shirt on and be the envy of their school. The only shirts that you should not sell (or charge a fee for) are your 1,000 Pound Club (refer to #23) and 1,200 Pound Club (refer to #24) shirts. Anything that a player *earns* is given to him. It is a reward for doing something outstanding.

When your reconditioned equipment is returned to you at the end of the year, you will have rejected helmets. Instead of discarding them, take out all of the padding, put a face mask on the helmet and sell it at your pre-season team sportswear store before your orientation meeting in August. Any used game jerseys that have been replaced by new ones can also be offered for sale to players and parents. You will see many of the parents wearing their son's jersey in the stands on game night. Sell these for a reduced rate so you can move them. Don't price yourself out of a sale. These items can be pure profit and will go right into your fundraising account.

10

Supervision of the Entire Program

The high school head football coach should have control of the varsity, sub-varsity, JV, freshman, and middle school football programs. Do not neglect your middle school program. If a school system does not have middle school football, it is one of the first things that a new head coach should lobby for. By overseeing all teams, the program's philosophy and "X's and O's" can be implemented as early as the sixth or seventh grade. Building loyalty to the high school program early in a player's career makes for a smooth transition from middle school to freshman or JV football at the high school. Then, as the head coach, you have the responsibility of being available to support the middle school coach.

Providing off-season instruction, helping to establish and run an off-season weight-lifting program, and including the middle school coaches in the high school staff meetings and attendance at clinics are all part of building the rapport that's necessary to establish the continuity from middle school to high school. It is important for you to be known by the middle school players and their parents. You need to attend middle school games, appear at the middle school post-season banquet, and show up for a Saturday pre-season practice.

The next step is recruiting. To generate interest in participating in the football program, invite students to join your off-season weight program. Hang out in the halls and talk to kids as they walk by. The important factor is to "be seen" talking to kids. Ask the track, wrestling, and basketball coaches if they would be interested in having their athletes lift with you in the football weight program. It may be in-season for these sports, but you could set up a program for them. Those wrestlers, runners, and jumpers are the guys you want to get interested in your football program. Starting them in your weight program is a great way to capture their interest. Many competitive activities can be presented to make them want to come back for more. Make it tough, but make it fun, and kids will want to join your program.

The weight program you run must be organized. The athletes must leave knowing that they worked hard and that they accomplished something. Just opening the room and letting them come in and do a few curls and lift on the bench is not sending the right message. You must know what you are doing and run your off-season program with the same intensity, organization, and enthusiasm as your regular-season practices.

Many programs have a nice three- to four-year run as a championship-level team and then when that group of athletes graduate, the team record slips back to mediocre. The key to long-term success is to always be thinking about *next* year. This philosophy may contradict the old adage of "don't think ahead to next week's opponent," but if you are not thinking about next year, it will arrive and you won't have the talent to sustain a high level of success. Always be thinking, *what can that underclassman do to help us next year?*

Two practices in particular can be utilized to act on this philosophy. First, never back up a senior starter with another senior. Find a legitimate underclassman who is not starting and work him at that position in practice every day. Take advantage of any opportunity to get the underclassman in the game when the game is still on the line. That same player will likely be lining up as the starter at that position in next year's opener. You want him to feel like he's "been there, done that" when the next season starts.

In practice, man your scout teams with those same underclassmen backups. If you have a sophomore, or even a freshman, who is skilled enough to make the varsity squad, he must "earn his stripes" on the scout team. Going up against the starting defense for 13 weeks makes a young man grow up and develop the mental and physical toughness that he needs to compete for that starting position next year. In particular, young running backs—even ones who were middle school stars—need a year of getting banged on in order to develop the confidence necessary to face varsity competition as a sophomore or junior. You'll notice the biggest turnarounds with offensive linemen. For example, it may take all season, but watch a big sophomore get beat on by a varsity defensive lineman every day, and you will see some remarkable advances in confidence and physical toughness. By the time he's a junior, he is ready to "dish it out" instead of taking it.

The second practice that reinforces the "always be thinking about *next* year" philosophy is to consider getting the younger players with the most potential on your varsity squad as soon as possible (depending on how your school system devises JV and varsity teams). At every level, from high school to college to pro, players have to have a "rookie season," when they are indoctrinated to the rigors of that particular level of ball. Get your best sophomore or even an outstanding freshman on the varsity and let him have that "rookie" season as early as possible in his high school career. He won't play as much as if you kept him down on the JV team where he would probably be a star, but that underclassman will gain valuable experience competing every day in practice against better competition than he'll ever see in a JV or sub-varsity game one night a week for seven to eight games.

Make it a rule that any sophomores on the varsity team *have* to get on the field, even if it's nothing more than a kicking team, to gain game experience. As they prepare for their junior year, they will already be veterans. They will be in much better position to compete for a starting position and, most importantly, you will have players who will be two-year starters and not "one-year wonders" as seniors.

One unwritten rule is if a player starts on our JV team as a freshman, he is usually ready to move up to varsity as a sophomore. If he starts on JV as a ninth-grader, he has accomplished all that our JV is designed to give and he needs to compete on the varsity as a 10th-grader. If a player or his parents balk at moving up, I ask them if the player successfully completed all his academic classes as a freshman. The answer is usually "yes." Then I talk it over with his teachers and his guidance counselor and suggest that it will be best if that player repeats his ninth-grade classes. With the incredulous look I get from the player or his parents, I respond with, "It's the same thing with his football. He's experienced success on the JV team by starting—he is ready to be promoted to the varsity." Most kids are very competitive if they like to play football. We make playing on the Varsity a player's primary goal as an incoming freshman. It is like going down to the minors in professional baseball if you were sent down to the JV team. The varsity got the new uniforms while the JV got the hand-me-downs. The varsity dressed in the nice locker room with the sound system. The JV dressed in an old converted public restroom in the stadium. Everything you do should be designed to make playing on the varsity the most appealing and important thing for a young player in your program to want to aspire to.

There are, no doubt, other factors and ideas that play into making your team successful. Great facilities are nice, but they aren't necessary to win championships. For instance, our locker room also served as our weight room for the first 20 years I was head coach. We called it "the pit." There was no air conditioning in the room and it was crowded, but we got a lot of good work done in there. Having nice uniforms and first-rate equipment, however, *is* important. It is a source of pride for your program. You want to look good and have your players well-protected when you take the field.

The talent level, as previously mentioned, is always important but it is more important to *develop* that talent than to just be blessed with a bunch of great athletes. Take a player with a little less ability who wants to work to be the best he can be and help him achieve his goals. It's the player who's loaded with talent (and knows it) that you have your work cut out with. Watch out for the players who are more concerned about the name on the back of their jersey (their own) than they are about the name on the front of their jersey (the team's).

Coaches should believe in and adhere to the old adage of "plan your work and work your plan." Hopefully, this book has provided some ideas that will help you when you start planning your work—ideas that perhaps you have never considered or even knew could help you be more successful. Nothing beats having talent. It's being able to utilize that talent to your utmost over a long period of time that will earn you the recognition of being a successful coach. Once you have your plan in place, work hard, work smart, and good things will happen.

These *"little things* that make a BIG difference" will hopefully help young coaches to have a more successful program. Once a tradition of excellence is established, it will become the bedrock of your program—one that will be recognized in your area as a program built on helping kids be the best they can be—on and off the field.

About the Author

Lew Johnston was the head football coach at Western Branch High School in Chesapeake, VA, for 22 years (following a 11-year stint as an assistant coach). His overall record as head coach was 163-64-3, including five southeastern district championships (1997, 2001, 2002, 2003, and 2006) and one eastern regional championship (2002). Lew was named southeastern district Coach of the Year six times (1991, 1995, 1997, 2001, 2002, and 2006) and was selected by the Virginia High School Coaches Association as the eastern region, division 6, Virginia Coach of the Year in 2002. The Portsmouth Sports Club (VA) honored him with its Abe Goldblatt Tidewater Scholastic Coach of the Year award in 1997, 2001, 2002, and 2006.

Lew retired from coaching high school football after the 2006 season, then returned to coaching in 2008, working with seventh and eighth graders for the first time as the head football coach at Jolliff Middle School (Chesapeake, VA), where he is also a guidance counselor. In his first year as head coach, his team was 7-0 and won the Chesapeake Middle School City Championship.

Lew earned a full football scholarship to The College of William and Mary in 1967, playing under Marv Levy and Lou Holtz. William and Mary was the Southern Conference champion in 1971 and played in the Tangerine Bowl in Orlando, FL. Lew graduated from William and Mary in 1971 with a BA in Psychology. Lew also holds a master's degree from Old Dominion University in education and counseling.

Lew and his wife, Nancy, have been married for 36 years. They have two children, Bryan and Amanda, and a granddaughter, Alex. He and his wife attend Village Christian Fellowship in Suffolk, VA, where he is an elder. His proudest accomplishment in coaching is that seven of his former players have been in full-time Christian ministry.